The Art of
Space Management

The Art of Space Management

Roni Oren

Translation from Hebrew: **Ed Codish**
Art: **Roni Oren**
Photography: **Uri David**

Copyright © 2011 by Roni Oren.
17a Harishonim, Hod Hashron, Israel.

Orenroni7@gmail.com
www.space-management-tc.com

All rights reserved. No part of this book may be reproduced, stored in a retrieval system, or transmitted in any form or by any means, electronics, mechanical, photocopying, recording, or otherwise, without the prior written permission of the author.

ISBN: 978-1479192076

Plates, printing and binding by Keterpress Enterprises, Jerusalem
Printed in Israel 2012

Contents

Introduction	7
The Need for a New Concept of Management	13
The Structural Architecture of the Space: Goals, Boundaries and Degrees of Freedom	35
The Social Psychological Architecture of Space: Holding and Containing	75
The Idea of the Vision in the Space Management Model	99
The Space Manager or The Functional Manager	111
Organizational Stories / Case Studies	129
The End	161

Introduction

Nothing in the first three decades of my life predicted that I would be a manager, and certainly not a manager in a corporate environment. My mother had been a teacher, and my father a small businessman who specialized in the incurring of large debts. My parents were cultured people who loved and appreciated art, and in our home they entertained important writers and artists. Then, I thought I would be a man of letters, an artist. I drew, I liked nature, I had a great love of music. I have played guitar since my youth. At the university, I studied psychology and philosophy and planned to continue in clinical psychology. When I received my BA in psychology, I applied to the Master's program in clinical psychology. Like many others, I was rejected. At that time, an opportunity in management opened for me, and since I was married and had two daughters, I decided on a path that would make us some money.

From my first encounter with the corporate world, I knew I was different. Often my decisions and style were not understood and so were opposed. My tendency to go into the psychological and philosophic depth of things, the way I envisioned organization and its methods, particularly those that were not conscious, sometimes caused a general unease. On the other hand, In every company I was leading Human Resources, HR achieved great success. This success was recognized by parties outside my employers when the human resources section of 'yes' under my direction won first prize for management of human resources for a project of organizational intervention in the door-to-door sales department in 2006. I describe this project in Chapter Six.

In the wake of this project, I wrote an article on space management in which for the first time I attempted to present my concepts of management. When I left 'yes', I decided to expand this article into a book. It took three years to write the book due to difficulties caused by the need to combine personal views of the world, intuition, beliefs, theoretical knowledge and the practice of management, and to convert this into a management model I could share with others.

At the center of the theory set forth in the book is the concept of "space." The connection of "space" to the world of management was given me by Yael, a manager at Soda Club's Human Resources. Yael asked me for freedom of action to apply her skills and knowledge and to clear a "space" for her in which to operate. She asked me to help her impart her expertise without interference from internal organizational politics or from any extraneous power struggles. She asked me to create for her the opportunity to devote her personal resources in order to advance the company's ability to fulfill its mission. In her own words: "I have a lot of professional knowledge but no strength for fights and conflicts. I don't need any assistance in matters of my profession, but I need a space I can influence. If you can make me that space, I'll take care of the rest."

I knew Yael and her professional abilities well and also recognized her difficulty with power struggles. From time to time she would come into my office, smile, and ask me to yell at someone who was holding her back. Yael's contributions to the operations at Soda Club were great. Later, she agreed to join me in moving to 'yes' and there, too, her contributions were great. I never had to "manage" her or to monitor her work, only to create a framework for her in which she could contribute, develop and advance. She never disappointed me. I understood that when I secured Yael the space in which she could operate, I was offering her both freedom and protection. I instilled in her the self-assurance she needed to exert influence and to assert her values and released her from the waste of energy involved in doubts and power struggles.

The concept of "space" and all that is associated with it has been part of me all my life. My first experience of "space" was implanted in me in early childhood in the Ramat Hasharon of the late 1950s and early 1960s. In those years Ramat Hasharon was a rural and somewhat neglected settlement. Very close to my house was a large grove of pine trees where I spent hours imagining adventures with Indians and the American Wild West, with Eskimos in the frozen Arctic, with horsemen on missions for the Czar in the wastes of Siberia. During summer vacation, when time stretched endlessly, I would ride my old bicycle to a distant eucalyptus grove. In that grove I followed birds and rabbits, turtles and hedgehogs, made bows and arrows from branches and spent more time in the branches than on the ground.

When I was ten we moved to Tel Aviv. The big city seemed stifling to me, and I longed for the spaces and landscapes we had left behind. So when I finished grammar school, I decided to study in the boarding school at Hakfar Hayarok, whose fields I remembered from my early childhood in Ramat Hasharon.

The agricultural school in Hakfar Hayarok yielded an experience of space different from that of my childhood. I still experienced space, but to that experience were added boundaries and rules. Besides the place's physical space, there was also a wide personal space. Pupils who played musical instruments could get a room for practicing and others who cared for animals received room for them. The school was open and nonjudgmental. There was little supervision and few borders, but those borders were well marked. The teachers and staff did not lord it over the students. The respect we received as children was real, not simply given as a matter of policy. Life at HaKfar Hayarok was not easy. Every day, we farmed for four hours in addition to learning a full school day, and we did not have the luxuries of home. We were expected to act as adults and were granted the freedom of adults. The combination of space, freedom, and boundaries made us independent agents in our minds and in our deeds, valuing work and willing to strive. Only after years of personal development and education did I understand what a great educator Mr. Gershon Zach, principal of the school during those years, was.

The next chapter in my life to influence me with the concept of space was my military service in Nachal, which combined military training and settlement on the land. The unit in which I served established the agricultural settlement of Zofar in the Arava, the long valley between the Dead Sea and the Gulf of Aqaba. We were a group of twenty nineteen-year-old men and women who found ourselves in the vast spaces of the Arava. We had a budget and had been allotted fifty acres on which to grow crops. We established a social framework and elected a treasurer and a coordinator. The moshav movement lent us an instructor who taught us management and budgeting and an agricultural instructor from Ein Yahav who taught us and advised us about crops and work methods. Otherwise, we were our own masters. We were completely responsible for our investments and the business results. We had to decide how many acres to plant in each crop, how to allot the workday, whether or not to work on the Sabbath, whether to harvest and market green tomatoes because prices were high or to wait two days and market them when they turned red.

The final chapter, which had a decisive influence on my concept of management, was the eight years I managed the human resources department of Soda Club, an international company in consumer goods. When I entered the company, the founder and CEO, Mr. Peter Weisberg, explained his business vision, the commercial structure of the company, and in general what my contribution towards the company's success was expected to be. Soda Club had started as a very small company, with a turnover of about eighteen million dollars and a hundred and fifty employees, but with a great vision. Peter Weisberg managed his organization with openness, and with the belief that given the right personnel, they would not have to be managed. His style of management manifested itself by need based management and individual meetings with him. Managers were free to do what they felt necessary to accomplish the company's goals. They were granted great influence and so made great contributions. Sometimes I felt there was too much freedom and the boundaries were unclear, but most of the time I derived great satisfaction from this. The company flourished at a dizzying pace and even overcame a deep business crisis and did this almost without centralized management control. During the eight years I worked there the company grew to a turnover of more than €120 million and employed eleven hundred people in countries around the world, among them Switzerland, Germany, Britain, the United States, Australia, and of course Israel. In many ways, and in particular because of the freedom the company gave its managers, I enjoyed this period in my career more than any other, and grew much as both person and manager. More recently, the company changed its name to Soda Stream and is listed on the American stock exchange.

They say a person is molded by the landscape of his birth. These three periods in my life, which I decided to describe in the introduction to this book, greatly influenced the way I chose to manage in the course of my career and they are my mold from nativity. The experiences of my life are the source of my desire for freedom in action and influence, the desire for personal liberty and growth without ceiling or blockages, and to my belief that an individual is obligated to personal freedom and growth. But we should not make the mistake of thinking that freedom, liberty and independence are easy. Erich Fromm wrote *Escape from Freedom* after World War II and offers us explanations of the anxiety freedom awakens in us and the human tendency to avoid freedom. Fromm shows how freedom to determine our destiny separates the individual from society he so much wants to be part of and makes him anxious. The fear leads him to reject freedom. Indeed, the personal and professional development and success of the individual cannot occur in comfortable areas in which everything is clear and there is no need for true freedom. Freedom means difficult choices and the assumption of responsibility and does not allow us to blame others for our failures and mistakes. Freedom requires that we be independent in our ideas and thoughts at all times. Freedom requires that we adopt no truth just because it is based on authority; we must doubt and question and of course we will make mistakes and pay for them. When we realize our freedom we cannot blame fate for our position in society and the world. My own path always depended on independent choices, with social distinctions and personal freedom, which was never easy, but I do not regret a moment of it.

I formed my personal management style from my own taste, my values, my beliefs and my experience. I believe that to be a high level professional or manager is not an appointment but a state of mind. In every position I held, I felt responsible to the company, and not just for my own missions. My identification with the company was always total, but I guarded my freedom to do what I believed was correct and my individuality as a person as well as a manager. I managed my way by an internal vision of the things or values that I wanted to accomplish for the organization during my tenure there. I always spurred people on to flourish, to grow and to succeed out of responsibility and freedom to influence and to work according to their beliefs. I always believed that a person, an organization, a society can accomplish more than they think they can if they are able freely to express themselves in their tasks. I learned to manage in unorthodox ways and I succeeded. Experience taught me that the more difficult the organization's challenges, and the more complex the organization's structure, my way had to be anti-management and had to give space for personal initiative and individual accomplishment.

Over the course of my years of work, I took part in a program of training in organizational consulting with a psychoanalytic-systemic approach, a joint program of "Ofek" and the Hebrew University. Through this approach, I became aware of the importance of observing the social and psychological processes that occur in an organization and the critical importance of managing the boundaries in an organization and adopted concepts from this methodology to form my own ideation. Over the last years I worked on conceptualizing and formulating a management method, which for me was intuitive, that could be learned, studied, and also imparted.

While I was working on this book, an unprecedented worldwide economic crisis occurred, and I understood that the method I present could illuminate important aspects in the world of management that contributed much to the recent collapse. I understood that current management practices of inspection and control have proven bankrupt and that my research may show the correct paths to take.

This book is also a space. At the bottom of each page I have left a place for the reader who reads actively to write his comments and ideas and so conduct a dialog with what is written. In this book you will find sayings and comments that are tentative, questions without answers, and a place for questions not yet posed. There is no absolute truth in this book. From beginning to end it is intellectual research and a personal experience, and like all thought and research, as they become deep, there will remain elements requiring further examination. You are invited to take part.

The Need for a New Concept of Management

In my professional career, I hardly ever dealt with management in the traditional sense of the word. I dealt with strategy, with teaching my people to think independently and in pattern-shattering ways, with implementing organizational values and with constructing the right positions for the human capital in the company. I hardly ever checked the performance of tasks. It was clear to me that if the tasks were not being done at the level and within the time I asked for, my people would make sure to let me know.

I think the basis for the management path I chose comes from two sources. One is my view of people and the world. For reasons not clear even to myself, and God is my witness that I did not take this in with my mother's milk, I chose to believe that humankind is essentially good and that, if given true space, will always choose to do the good and the beneficial. To the same extent I have also always believed that the world is filled with opportunities. Given that I am a relatively sane person, it was clear to me that despite my beliefs not everyone is trustworthy and that the world contains more than a few dangers. However, I've trusted that my intuition would help me note the dangers and avoid them and the people not worthy of trust. These basic beliefs became the basis on which I constructed my approach.

Space for comments & insight

Formal academic learning, informal learning, and a great deal of curiosity and willingness to experiment, err and learn, soon accompanied these very basic and personal foundations. At the university, of course, I chose to study those things that supported by beliefs, and because of my love for my own personal freedom, my nonconformist positions and unusual thinking, I chose to grant my people the freedom and right to think for themselves without having to pay a personal cost for their differing views.

However, my own personal taste and beliefs, which have undoubtedly been relevant for me in writing a book about management, are but one necessary though insufficient anchor. It is therefore important to look at change in the business world, in society and in individuals, and point to those changes with which one turns what could remain simply in the realm of a personal management style into a developmental necessity in the world of management.

Why new concept of management is needed? – evolution, not revolution

Management has existed as a profession for only about one hundred years, a hundred years in which revolutionary changes have occurred in science and technology, economics and society, which are barely grasped by human consciousness. To point out the rate of change, the reader is invited to consider that the first time a person was able to control a plane and fly – for less than a minute – was the Wright brothers' flight in 1903.

Management as a profession began with the theories of Frederick Taylor, who is considered the father of scientific management and one of the fathers of

Space for comments & insight

management in general. An essay he published in 1911 is considered the cornerstone in the history of management. His central thesis was that a worker is interested in selling his labor at the highest price while investing minimal effort, and that he would prefer to work at conventional tasks in a well-known environment so as to avoid surprises. He also claimed that the work procedures must be detailed, clear, constant and known in advance, so that there would be very little for the worker to decide. The quality of performance would be determined by norms, which could be measured. Two decades later, the psychologist Elton Mayo developed an approach to managing human resources that stressed concern for the emotional needs of the employee, and in contrast to Taylor, who saw the efficiency of the worker as dependent on pay and on proper motivation by the manager, Mayo found a correlation between concern for the worker's emotional needs and his productivity.

Many theories of management were written and tested over the course of the century since the development of the foundations of scientific management and human resource management. Schools of thought rose and fell. Sometimes they did not meet their own requirements, sometimes they made partial contributions, and sometimes they provided ideas and concepts, a language and a prism through which organizational processes could be seen. Among the schools whose conceptions became part of the language of the world of management it is worth noting the approach of Professor Ichak Adiges first published in 1976 in an essay in *California Management Review* and in his book *How to Solve the Mismanagement Crisis*. Another doctrine that contributed its idea was that of Dr. Eliyahu M. Goldart who developed the "theory of constrains" that dealt mainly with resources on production lines. His best-known book is *The Goal*, written in the 1980s. To these approaches may be added that of Kaizen, born in Japan, who contributed

Space for comments & insight

to the world of management "quality cycles" that were meant to introduce continuous improvements to an organization. When considering the degree of relevance of the different concepts of management, it is necessary to take into account the time in which they were developed. No matter how good and enlightening these concepts, their power will fade when the times change. In the framework of my career as a manager, which has extended over twenty years, I have worked in public service and in heavy industry, in an international company dealing in consumer products, and in a communications firm. Over the course of my life I have encountered a variety of management styles, some of which arose from the nature of the company and others out of the personalities of the managers. I became aware that despite rapid changes in the world of commerce and in society, the culture of management and the doctrines of management are still ties to the value bases of the conception of scientific management of the old industries and still depend on, control, inspection and efficiency.

In organizations where control, inspection and efficiency were not relevant, and absent of alternative to traditional management, a permissive management culture developed that made only the immediate "bottom line" sacrosanct, a culture lacking boundaries, where everything is permissible as long as the bottom line benefits. This culture of management has time and again led to the collapse and implosion of a bubble, until the current great economic crisis that began in 2008.

Naturally enough, the world of management has reached a point where it is necessary to effect an essential change. It must be adapted to the pace and character of the current era and the era we will soon approach. The time has come to slough off the style of management that is still a derivative, however advanced, of the scientific management a la Taylor and instead grow a new,

Space for comments & insight

flexible skin. The organization towards which we are working in our social, economic and human development does not need more task management and its people do not need more of the constant command and control, but rather management of its goals, structure and freedom. Such an organization, built as an open system, would allow the people working in it to grow and flourish as individuals and enrich the organization much, much more than any organizational structure that preceded it and would improve its ability to adapt to a frequently changing reality.

The changes in the social and organizational environment

An important change in the social and organizational environment affecting the nature of the type of management necessary is a change in the nature of all of the systems: from the family, through the schools, to the economic, industrial and political systems. A world that was entirely constructed of closed systems – systems of continuity and tradition – has become a world of open systems affecting and affected by every change in the environment. The concept of "open systems" comes from biology, but was adopted by psychology and then organizational psychology. A closed system is one that is not affected by external influences unless these are extreme. A public organization, such as a municipality or a government office, does not change unless there is a crisis that forces it to change. Productive companies in the field of heavy industry operate like closed systems and manufacture more and more of the same thing, while wearing out both machinery and workers. As long as there is no catastrophe, companies will continue to use the same patterns of action. When workers and machines get worn out, others that will continue to produce more and more of the same product replace them.

Space for comments & insight

Such systems do not adapt to a changing reality until, suddenly, one day, they stop being relevant and cease to exist. Such systems are characterized by the fact that their workers do the same job for decades, from the day they enter the organization until they retire. The managers hold all knowledge, and that knowledge is valid for many years. Management is local and is oriented to the past: what was true in the past and proved itself then is therefore the basis for decision making in the present and future. Creativity, initiative, self-fulfillment, if it exists – all of these are reserved for the very senior management, or for the few in research and development. In such closed systems the most important things for workers are seniority and experience. To this day, the compensatory systems of such organizations still reward employees by incremental salary increases for every year of seniority simply for the fact that they've been with the company for many years, the assumption being that seniority equals experience and is therefore itself a value. In such systems, change is threatening and very difficult to effect.

My first job as a manager in the industrial sector was with Dead Sea Periclase Ltd., which manufactures raw materials for the steel smelter industry. The company was a profitable one and controlled its target market, but the system itself was rigid and slow. A strong employee committee prevented management from operating freely in response to market needs.

The steel industry for which the company made its products was shrinking. The need for steel in the automotive industry was dropping as the result of improvements in the efficiency of steel manufacturing and with the introduction of alternate amalgams and the market was becoming increasingly competitive. Despite the high quality of the products at Periclase, market economics were dictating lower prices. Periclase was finding it hard to compete in price because of the high costs of energy and labor. The company worked to

Space for comments & insight

save on energy but was unable to reduce labor costs required for production. To the best of my memory, when I was the company's HR manager, labor costs represented some 40% of the product price. I have to admit that I took important part in the formulation and signing of contracts that preserved these labor costs. Perhaps if the company had reduced the cost of labor it would have had the tools to handle better the competition and it would not have been forced to close production lines and fire workers. By contrast, public systems do not operate in a competitive marketplace and are therefore unaffected by fluctuations in "the real world." Therefore the chance that they will experience a catastrophe that will force them to change is very small. As long as there is no privatization, they will remain a monopoly.

The treasury, the National Insurance Institute or the Department of Motor Vehicles will operate as closed systems and resist transformation as long as they have no competition on the free market, just as the Israel Electric Company is not required to change a thing because it makes the consumer pay for all market vagaries. When it cannot provide enough electricity it initiates brownouts and when the cost of the "product" goes up it raises the price the consumer pays. By contrast, Bezeq Communications, the leading land line communications company in Israel, was forced to become an open system the day the telephone marketplace invited competition. The employees in companies that function as closed systems usually have less education and versatility and possess narrower fields of expertise derived from working many years in the same position. Worker turnover is very low; employees who lose their place in such systems will have a hard time finding a job elsewhere. The welfare and compensatory apparatus in these closed systems are not linked to personal performance.

Today's world of business and production, especially manufacturers of technological, communications and financial products, is part of a completely

Space for comments & insight

different solar system where all commercial systems are open. A manufacturer cannot allow itself to produce the same product over and over because it will lose its market share within a couple of years. Moreover, many companies are now making products that are from the outset not meant to last over time because the next generation of technology is already in the pipeline. Whatever knowledge we possessed a year or two ago is irrelevant for tomorrow. The value of an employee is not measured in experience but rather in his or her ability to learn new topics and technologies quickly, and apply creativity and initiative. We are constantly involved in looking at market trends and technology in order to identify the future towards which we are steering the organization; management has become future oriented. In between closed and open systems there are also hybrids, where the development and marketing structure represents a very open system whereas the manufacturing structure bears the marks of a closed one. I assume (with all due respect and caution) that Teva Ltd., the world leader in generic pharmaceuticals and the patent holder for Copaxon, incorporates open and closed systems. The marketing and research, strategy, finances, trade and similar structures would tend to be more open than the company's production plants.

Companies that were founded as open or became so with time typically produce products (whether physical products or services) with short life spans, and tend to be based on high degrees of innovativeness, decentralization and globalization. Employees of companies operating as open systems are highly skilled and educated, have a high degree of versatility and are very much in demand in the job market. Turnover of employees in such companies is fairly high as is the companies' dependence on key personnel. Such companies have developed welfare and compensatory systems that are directly linked to employees' personal performance. Thes companies have sophisticated recruitment structures, and a HR management with a central role to play.

Space for comments & insight

The table below presents the main differences between open and closed organizations:

Parameter	Closed systems	Open systems
Business environment	Stable and slow environment. High consumer loyalty, slow degradation of product (long life span), low level of competition; stable profit margins.	Quick pace, low consumer loyalty, very competitive. Rapid degradation of product, decreasing levels of profitability through product's life span.
Organizational flexibility	Rigid organization with organizational mechanisms blocking change (institutionalized work culture).	Flexible organization that responds rapidly, a mechanism favoring change (R&D unit work culture)
Innovation	Hardly exists, except for units in charge of product development. Management culture based on employee experience. i.e., past oriented management.	Innovation is key: the past is of no interest. The moment a product is launched the company focuses on the next one. Most employees are involved in the innovation, both in development and service. i.e., future oriented management.
Values	Loyalty, routine, consistency and experience, long terms of employment, seniority, tradition, nostalgia.	Frequent changes, short terms of employment, looking to the future, initiative, frenetic pace.
Authority	Notable hierarchy, obedience, command and control; authority is also expertise.	Moderate hierarchy based on professional expertise and moderate obedience; employees often possess more expertise than their managers.

Social changes

Until the 1980s, people's lives were typically stable for years at a time. Social norms sanctified perseverance and personal sacrifice by the breadwinner on behalf of his family. Career changes, business adventures and search for self-fulfillment were considered rash and irresponsible. Steady job in companies – preferably in banks, the public service sector, or in government companies – were seen as highly desirable. The most important things were tenure and pension, even if you were in your twenties. When I was a teen, many of my contemporaries were sent to trade schools in order to learn a profession. Personal development and the broadening of horizons were never even mentioned. One's personal expression, self-realization, or the fulfillment of talents, were seen as the luxuries of the idle and rich. However, in the last two decades, it is evident that the need for space for personal growth, influence, fulfilling dreams and self-expression has undergone reevaluation. Many psychologists have dealt with different human needs, from the basic existential ones to such as self-fulfillment. The best-known researcher whose theories are studied in many management courses is Abraham Maslow. His Hierarchy of Needs diagram shows the human motivational mechanism as he understood it in the years in which he developed it (1943-1954). Maslow defined a pyramid of needs of five steps

1. At the base of the pyramid are the physiological needs, including food and shelter, and these are the foundation for all other needs. A person who experiences insufficiencies in fulfilling such a need, says Maslow, will risk his or her life in order to fulfill it.
2. The next step is the need for physical safety, which people will try to secure only once their physiological needs have been met. This means that someone whose belly is full, for example, will be available to defend him/herself from other dangers

Space for comments & insight

3. After the physiological needs and physical safety have been assured, Maslow's theory focuses on the need for social belonging.
4. The need for social esteem is a more elevated need: people seek to belong to society but also want to be valued and respected by it.
5. Finally comes the need for self-actualization, the drive to realize personal capabilities, a need seen by Maslow as the ultimate need, though of course attempting to fill this need depends on one's ability to fill all the other, more basic, needs.

Clayton Alderfer further developed Maslow's theory and sorted needs into three basic categories:

1. Physical existence – in its absence, social belonging is less important to people.
2. Social belonging – people may at times be prepared to subsume their own individuality and personal growth for its sake.
3. Personal growth – the highest need, one to which people will attend only when the previous needs in the hierarchy of needs have been met.

Alderfer, in developing his own model of motivation, was innovative in claiming that when a higher need is unmet people will regress and over-compensate with a lower need. I certainly saw evidence of this at Dead Sea Periclase Ltd., where people were trapped in a gilded cage. The more talented and capable they were, the more bitter and demanding they grew. Every reality check showed that their compensation was obviously higher than any compensation their skills would have brought them in any other setting. But the fact that they were unable to actualize their individuality frustrated them more and more. We, as managers, are familiar with the phenomenon when we take onboard overqualified people and the frustration they build up as a result. The lack of opportunity for personal

Space for comments & insight

growth within the organization will amplify the preoccupation with status, status symbols and unremitting demands for compensation.

Today, more so than in the past, working with greater operational and professional freedom is possible, even necessary. Together with the dramatic changes that have taken place in the standard of living and technology, there are been concomitant changes in education, general knowledge, patterns of thinking and individual abilities. And, together with these changes, our ability to conduct ourselves in spaces that provide freedom has also improved. If, in the past, many were content with a job that provided for their families' and their own basic necessities, today people also want their jobs to provide for personal and professional growth as well as self-actualization. I have interviewed thousands of job applicants and have had conversations with hundreds of managers. Almost all identified their need to matter, to be unique and to have an impact as a parameter more important than salary. If we adopt Alderfer's theory of needs, we understand that when those are not expressed, there will be a regression and a demand for compensation in the realms of physical existence and social belonging or status, i.e., the symbols of status and money. The new type of employee wants a place for him/herself that is separate and distinct from the group to the same extent that s/he wants to belong, and may even be prepared to pay a price in the degree of belonging if only s/he can realize him/herself as an individual. The combination of these observations of people's needs and their attempts to fulfill them as well as my own experience indicate that organizations that do not respond to people's need to actualize their human capital will have to come up with a more serious response to people's more basic needs in the form of salaries and status symbols. This organization will experience pointless political maneuverings designed to create a false sense of prominence to some of their personnel. And, more than that, such organizations will hold back the actualization of the tremendous potential for achievement inherent in human capital.

Space for comments & insight

Human capital

The development of humans in the West has led to high levels of education and skills; people's contribution has become more significant and their freedom to choose a job in accordance with their needs and desires has grown. This change has obligated employers to provide a response to developmental needs, such as improving their employees' professional status and academic training and becoming more attractive to them. The personnel management approach no longer sufficed and developed into the human resources approach. The HR approach focuses on people's deeper needs that go beyond making a living and providing for their physical existence; it seeks to respond to needs relating to personal and professional development. Programs for developing managers, workshops on interpersonal relations, academic studies financed by the company – all are part of the innovation generated by this approach. But human potential doesn't stop there. Recent decades have placed at our doorstep people with significantly higher abilities than what was common a generation ago: their nature is different and they have a higher drive to realize their human capital.

Thomas O. Davenport, in *The Human Capital: What It Is and Why People Invest It*, presents a model of human capital as well as a principle for relating to human capital. According to Davenport, human capital is the employee's property, and only the employee decides where and how much to invest it. The following diagram presents the structure of layers comprising human capital on the basis of accessibility and the degree of influence an organization has over them

The diagram proposes that the organization has a great deal of say in managing time at work and a lot of influence on the worker's conduct

---

Space for comments & insight

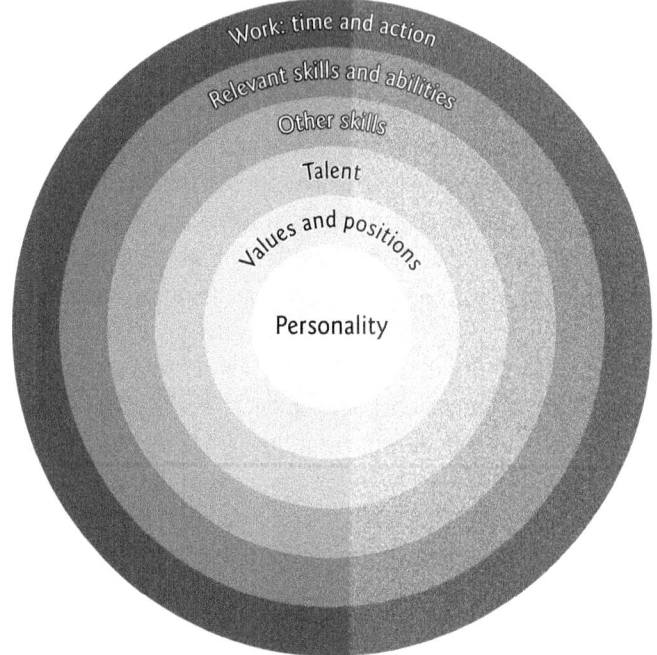

Layers of Human Capital

and relevant skills, whether acquired for the worker by the company or acquired in previous positions and professional training. In companies that deal with creation and development one may assume that talent will also find expression in the day-to-day work, though it is located in a layer that cannot be managed. The deeper layers cannot, in fact, be managed and the organization's access to them is very limited. Nevertheless, in proper management of the working environment, company managers can create

Space for comments & insight

the space in which employees and managers will want to and be able to express their maximal human capital.

The level of employees' performance rises exponentially when they have a place in the organization, a space for themselves and their skills and where they can express layers of their existence in the job place. The more employees feel that their contribution and impact are greater, the greater their involvement and investment will be. Therefore, an organization that makes sure to provide spaces in which its employees can express themselves and have an effect will discover that every office holder adds values that were not accessible or available to the organization earlier.

During my professional career I often ran into a gap between the expectations of the organization where I was working and my desire and need to act and have an impact. My career was never easy, mostly because I didn't do as I was told but rather what I thought was the right thing to do. I chose my own list of priorities. I saw myself as someone who owes an explanation to my clients, not only to my supervisors. This is not a simple statement. It would seem to be my supervisors' job to bear responsibility whereas I am supposed to do what they tell me. However, at times, I found that what I was told to do wasn't really important and designed some times to please someone in the chain of command; at other times, it even seemed to me that the instructions or requests stood in stark contradiction to the good of the organization. In such situations, I felt responsible for making a move I believed to be right for the company. On the basis of insights culled from my experience and according to the management approach that presents a model in which employees and managers actualize their human capital and bear responsibility, I would like to make a distinction between responsibility and accountability and guide the reader towards the value inherent in human capital specifically within circles of responsibility.

Space for comments & insight

Responsibility and accountability

Given the rapidly changing business and industrial world, the growing potency of human capital, and the development of personal knowledge and the decentralization of expertise to many jobs in an organization, a new way of looking at the question of accountability and responsibility in the organization is needed. Without going into fine formulations and the shaded meanings of the words "responsibility" and "accountability" available in the dictionary and professional literature, I would like to characterize these concepts for the sake of the management philosophy presented herein.

The organization defines jobs and units on the basis of an a priori view of the product required, and the accountability of the employees and managers is towards the product required from the field in which they work. A production line worker is hired in order to perform predefined actions in the process of putting some device together. The machine engineer is supposed to solve problems in the field of activity for which he was recruited or to develop processes the company has already planned. Closed systems typically focus on accountability of worker and manager. The organization's system of measurement, its performance control and assessment of performance, are supposed to measure and reward the worker and manager for meeting their commitment. Accountability can be defined as providing a response to a set of external expectations that define the product the manager and worker are supposed to produce. The realm of accountability is a very comfortable one in which to operate.

Space for comments & insight

The greater the success in it the more the organization's positive feedback and compensation also grow. By contrast, the realm of responsibility is one that may be much less comfortable and success may actually arouse opposition within the organization. Obviously, the responsibility of a worker or manager includes being accountable for the product, as a basic condition for the job. However, in my understanding of space management, this condition is necessary but not enough; the worker also bears responsibility. Without a comprehensive view of the organization's needs and the willingness to take risks and act where having an effect is possible, the employee is not fulfilling responsibility.

Similar to accountability, organizational responsibility of managers and workers lies in the field of work or activity of the individual but it exceeds the limits of accountability to the product and into the realm of impact. These areas of responsibility and impact are not comfortable and will not necessarily be rewarded by the organization. At times, the opposite is in fact the case. An HR coordinator who is supposed to recruit ten salespeople every month and handle the processes of ten other salespeople resigning or being terminated will receive positive feedback from the organization as long as she manages this task. The day she starts interviewing managers in order to understand the reasons for salespeople resigning or being fired, or interviews the salespeople leaving to understand their reasons for doing so and interviews workers staying within the system and looks for the answer to why ten people resign or are fired every month, she may indeed be seen as a disruptive element. Below is an illustration of the set of relations between human capital in all its varied layers and the circles of accountability and responsibility:

Space for comments & insight

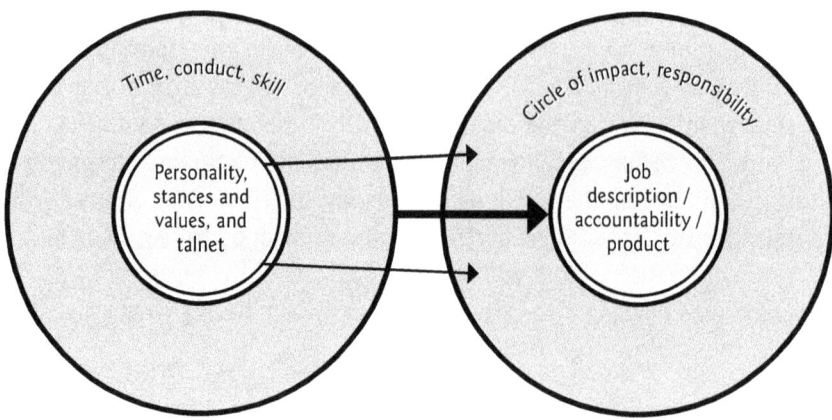

Relationship between human capital and responsibility and accountability.

The diagram shows the relationship between the layers of human capital and responsibility and accountability. The layers relevant to accountability do not necessarily require the involvement of all of someone's human capital. The layers of conduct, time invested in the work, skills relevant to the job and perhaps even talent, are enough to fulfill a person's accountability in his or her job. The inner circle of human capital, where the organization has almost no reach, is the human capital required in order to operate in the broader and more significant circle of the job, and that is the circle of responsibility and impact. Here, people operate in a system where their personality, talents and values find expression. People operating out of the deeper layers out of a high degree of personal involvement, out of a sense of commitment, and great responsibility, will actualize all of their human capital. Their contribution to the organization will be immeasurably greater.

Space for comments & insight

In this book, I propose a model for management in organizations structured as open systems and that adapt themselves constantly according to rapidly changing circumstances. In such organizations, each and every worker plays a role whose importance cannot be overstated. Every worker must be involved and flexible and take responsibility, not just for the sake of self-actualization but primarily to move the organization forward and allow it to meet the changing tasks. The complexity of managing such an organization places a great deal of responsibility and accountability on the worker, sometimes to a degree almost indistinguishable from the manager's. I believe that the key to proper management is, above all, freedom – freedom in the sense of autonomy to act and to make an impact, freedom that allows for the expression of human capital and human needs, freedom to develop and mature, personally and professionally, the freedom of adults. We are in the midst of this developmental process. The model I am proposing will show people in organizations a clear path for growing into the maximal degree of freedom they can actualize within the space in which they operate.

Space for comments & insight

The Structural Architecture of the Space: Goals, Boundaries, and Degrees of Freedom

In the previous chapter I asserted that a management model is needed that enables employees to contribute to the maximum their human capital inherent in them, while taking responsibility and influencing the organization. This model rests on a space that has rules and principles. We may point out five central elements that create an organizational space. Three of these are structural: goals, boundaries, and degrees of freedom, and two other are social psychological elements of holding and containing. Together, these elements unite into a management model whose principles are clear and can be learned and applied.

The Organizational Space

When we think of the idea of "space,"* we imagine wide fields and open valleys. For some it triggers pictures of the deserts or the sea. The idea of space arouses associations of uncrowded areas, with distant borders. The idea of open spaces generally arouses feelings of excitement and positive energy, a feeling of happiness, and certainly awakens our imagination. But just as it is possible to experience space as something tempting, exciting and joyful, it is also possible to experience it as threatening, dangerous and oppressive. A picture of a lone man in a blazing endless desert or in waves of the sea with no land in sight, a picture of a man in polar snow fields or in

---

* The Hebrew word translated here as "space" (*merhav*) generally refers to an expansive, three-dimensional, open place.

Siberia, immediately arouses in us feelings of helplessness, loneliness, and existential danger and of being lost. Just like the spaces of landscape and nature, so organizational space may, under certain circumstances be enticing, exciting and experiential, but under other circumstances can be threatening. The organizational space can, on the one hand, encourage people to action and assuming responsibility; it can on the other hand arouse in them anxiety, and a feeling that they have lost their way and purpose.

An organization is a "meta-space" divided into subordinate spaces. The organization may be commercial or public service. Spaces in the organization are identified by divisions such as sections, departments and teams, by means of positions and their job descriptions, and by tasks given to either an individual or to a group of people. In this chapter we will deal with the architecture of the space and the structural elements: goals, boundaries, and degrees of freedom.

The Goal of the Space

The goal of the space is the reason for its existence and the primary task of the people operating in it is to achieve that goal within the boundaries of the space. An entrepreneur, owners of a firm, founders of an NGO, an ideological body or a political party, as their first act in creating space define their goals. Without articulation of the space's goal, actions will lack direction. A child in a playground may act as if he has goals, and may even assign himself temporary goals, such as moving a pile of sand from one place to another, or to swing higher than he has before, but each action remains isolated and will not result in action that is focused. The goal of a space may be the fulfillment of a statesman's vision for the next decades or instead the acquisition of

Space for comments & insight

knowledge needed to use new software. The difference between these lies in the breadth they offer. The more the goal is limited or focused, the smaller the space.

I use as an imaginary example a goal placed before the research and development unit of a drug company. When the Board of Directors of a company that develops medicines, needs to articulate the goal for the R&D group it tends to identify goals very widely. The Board of Directors, whose interests are not scientific, medical or social, but rather economic, needs no in-depth knowledge of the expertise of the development team in the company; for that the company employs the Research & Development division manager. All that is required from that level of management is a correct definition of the objective that will create direction and the allocation of resources. Thus, the goal set may be, "Development of a drug that will be revolutionary in the world of medicine and become the best-selling drug in the world." The manager of the R&D division, who has a better knowledge of the research capabilities and human capital, may set a more limited goal such as "Discovery of a drug that prevents colon cancer." The manager of the section dealing with the development of anti-cancer drugs has in depth knowledge of studies already carried out in the division on colon cancer and is likely to narrow down and focus the goal to something like discovery of an enzyme that improves the ability of the cells in the body's digestive tract to overcome cancer cells. The manager of the research team may narrow down the target even further. This example is of course meant to be only illustrative. But we see that each decision reduces the degrees of freedom of the next level. If the executive board would decide that the goal is to develop a drug that prevented the occurrence of cancer of the colon, this would immediately eliminate the space of the manager of the R&D division and that of the manager of the section for developing anti-cancer drugs. There is no doubt that both goals are broad

Space for comments & insight

and very important but the first and wider formulation allows the scientists greater room for decision making. We can say that the more broadly a goal is expressed, the greater the possibility for creativity in its achievement and the less predictable the results are.

The goal is the North Star of the space, and its articulation is the key factor in the ability of those working on it to be effective. When this star's light is hidden in many other lights or fog those working in that space are liable to wander great distances in wrong directions without being aware of this. The goal of the space is also the yardstick to the value of any action. This all sounds clear and obvious but in practice very few managers concern themselves with these things, on the mistaken assumption that the goals are obvious. When looking at jobs ads on the Internet or in a newspaper we can see that the tasks of the position are given but the goals of the position are unknown and have probably never been formulated.

A few years ago I arranged a meeting with a team in the IT section of the company I worked at. Among those attending the meeting was an industrial engineer, part of whose job was to generate reports on manpower and labor costs for the customer care division. As part of an improvement in the report system of HR I wanted to reduce the exposure of data on personal salaries. I asked the engineer what purpose the reports serve, so as to understand if this proposed new way of data processing, which give the group costs without giving all the individual salaries, would still fulfill the purpose of the report. To my surprise, she did not know how the internal customers used the data, and in what resolution they needed the information. The engineer knew exactly what was required of her and performed this excellently, but did not at all know the goals, or how the data was being used, and thus could not use her judgment. I do not want to judge the engineer. In many organizations

Space for comments & insight

employees at various levels receive assignments in which, for them, the goal is to finish the assignment. Thus, if difficulties arise, they cannot use their judgment and make changes accordingly. More than this, if they receive faulty instructions they cannot assess them as faulty and protect the organization from mistakes. In order for someone working in a space to contribute real value, to use judgment and to invest his or her human capital, the person must have a clear understanding of the process he or she is part of and a clear understanding of his or her contribution to the process. Therefore, the first and most important job of the manager of a space is to guarantee that every employee always understands the goals of action. If the goals of the space are clear the need to manage the employees lessens and even disappears. The goals manage the operations of the space. Our obligation as managers is to identify exactly the goals of the space and to help the employees to identify completely their own goals.

Goals are defined in two circles (see Chapter 1): goals within the circle of daily accountability and functioning, and goals within the circle of responsibility entailing long-term actions and impact on the organization.

Goal Articulation Within the Circle of Accountability

The process of articulating goals within the circle of accountability is the simpler of the two, because the requirement for action comes from the client, whether internal or external, whose demands are usually clear. A technical support unit may, for example, not necessarily have to define goals within the circle of accountability because its clients will do so for it - an installation that doesn't work, a system whose products are defective, production equipment that is slower than it is supposed to be – all of these generate goals that are

Space for comments & insight

the default. A system of employee recruitment of service representatives in a communications company must meet its recruitment goals and the unit providing training for these recruits must also meet the goals of the training. Should these fail in their tasks; the service unit will not be able to answer the company's service calls. Failure to meet the routine goals in any one of these spaces will result in failures in other spaces and the organization will respond immediately. In such a situation, the Vice-President for Service will report on increased waiting times in phone responses or on a lower quality of response and explain this as being the result of the recruitment's and training's failure in attaining their goals. These goals, in the circle of accountability, are goals coming from outside the space. They were defined by internal or external clients.

However, even in the circle of accountability we need precise formulation of goals, or we are liable to find ourselves operating much like a kid in a sandbox, responding to ad-hock targets without directions.

I would like to invite you, the reader, to examine with me the definition of goals of the most junior position in the company that provides you with your mobile phone service, i.e., the customer service representative. The tasks of the customer service rep include answering customer calls and providing customers with accurate professional responses while creating a sense of satisfaction with the level of the service and the product. But having said that, have we really defined the goals of the job within that job description? Is customer satisfaction the goal? If we tell reps that the goal is customer satisfaction, they will not limit the time spent on the call or the benefits heaped on the customer. Do the shareholders really care about any particular customer's satisfaction? It is safe to assume that they are much more interested in customers continuing to pay for service over many years with less and less investment on the part of the company. Such an accurate

Space for comments & insight

definition would clarify for customer service representatives that while maintaining customer satisfaction they have to consider its cost, i.e., limit the time they spend on the call.

As a derivate of the goal – maintaining customer satisfaction and lowering the costs of service – the company may decide it is interested in developing an alternative form of service, via the Internet for example, in order to reduce the scope of incoming calls to customer call centers. This requires another change in the articulation of the goal, which would result in a respective change in the conduct of the customer service representatives. Such an articulation could be, "Maintaining customer satisfaction while directing customers to our Internet service." The newly articulated goal would justify extending the conversation for the sake of selling the electronic service. I recently contacted my insurance company in order to clarify the status of my policies. The customer service representative gave professional, courteous service, and the process of clarification lasted about 10 minutes. At the end of the conversation, having ascertained that I had received all the answers I needed, she suggested I register for service on the company's website where I would be able to learn the status of my policies without regard for the operating hours of the customer call center and without needing to wait for a customer service rep. Of course, I was happy to learn of this option and from now both the company and I will be spared the time and bother. In order to reach this desirable result, which has positive significance for the insurance company's profitability over time, the service rep had to extend the call by a few minutes. Clarifying the goals, its precise formulation, and its constant updating over time, is a critical parameter in the employee's and the manager's ability to fine tune their actions. The more complex a job is and the more impact it has, more managerial attention is required to define and articulate its goals.

Space for comments & insight

Goal Articulation at the Circle of Responsibility

Goals in the circle of responsibility are not imposed by anyone. Often organizations prefer not to deal with them at all. Managers are liable to have to pay a personal price on the road to achieving them. Thus one may ask: from where do the goals at the circle of responsibility derive? The only answer I have is: from responsibility for the general good of the organization over time. I deliberated over including the company's shareholders as those who articulate the responsibility of the officeholder, but my experience tells me that it's not that simple. At times, shareholders' interests differ and they do not always view the general good of the company as a goal. At times, company owners may demand that managers act in a certain way as the result of caprice or a hidden agenda or even out of a lack of professional understanding about the significance of their directives. At times, company owners acquire the concern only in order to raise its stock exchange value and then proceed to strip it of assets not given to monetary quantification, such as human capital and brand values. Therefore, the manager's responsibility is to the general good of the company over time. Clearly, I recognize that this definition is very problematic because it is unclear who identifies the general good for the officeholder. The answer is: no one. Therefore, responsibility is a very heavy burden, just as freedom is. People in senior positions in an organization may encounter dilemmas when accountability relating to their jobs and within their purview in the company collide with accountability in a forum they belong to, such as the management or the Board of Directors. In these jobs the distinction between goals in the circle of accountability and the goals in the circle of responsibility can be tricky.

An example of a collision between the two circles of accountability comes from the world of sales. At times, success in meeting the sales goal, the

---

Space for comments & insight

accountability of the sales manager in his or her job, may necessitate an agreement to acting in the gray area of sales representatives. Such activity is liable to damage the good name of the company and the manager's commitment as a company board member. Another example could be a dilemma faced by the CFO of a company. As the person in charge of the organization's finances, s/he is asked to supervise the organization's expenditures and reduce them as much as possible to present a picture of greater profitability. As such, s/he may oppose making investments in infrastructures, such as information systems, something that would negatively impact immediate business results as reflected by the profit-loss statement. At the same time, the CFO could be convinced that, without spending money on computer systems, the company is liable to find it increasingly difficult to compete in its market segment and therefore, as a result of her/his accountability as a board member s/her must support the investment required in information systems. Here, too, there is a collision between accountability as CFO and accountability as a board member.

Every manager responding to the organization's daily needs and efficiently creating the outputs expected of him/her will be considered an excellent manager. Such a manager can work through a full term in office without leaving an imprint on the organization and still be considered excellent. By contrast, a manager who sees organizational processes that, in his/her opinion, damage the organization's abilities and worth, processes that do not match the organizational goal and do not contribute towards it, and takes the initiative and tries to affect these processes and steer them, may arouse an entire chain over and develop covert organizational opposition. One could say that goals in the circle of responsibility will usually entail personal discomfort in a struggle to affect the path, growing difficulties as success is approached, and a high personal cost, especially in case of failure.

Space for comments & insight

Later in this book I will deal with the figure of the space manager and his/her ability to steer a course regardless of the social consensus, to contain organizational rejection, and even pay a personal cost for doing so. The goals in the circle of responsibility and the tasks derived from them that an officeholder adopts are not to be found in the comfort zone of accountability. Many times in my career I assumed responsibility and led unpopular moves no one believed in, except me. At times, I found myself fighting an organizational move tooth and nail, and more than once was I ready to leave an organization should boundaries be crossed, as was the case with Dead Sea Periclase when the labor council accrued unreasonable power and my attempts to moderate that power were not supported. Articulating goals in the circle of responsibility is complex and tough and entails no guarantees or clear indices of success. In one organization where I headed human resources, company managers were very focused on their personal status and less so on doing their jobs. Managers insisted on participating in meetings even when they weren't really contributing anything and stopped processes if those were taking place without their involvement. The organization wasted time, energy and management attention on putting together clever PowerPoint presentations and holding well-attended meetings that produced little of value. I assume that this picture is familiar to managers in many organizations. At a certain point, many managers started to demand the creation of an additional managerial layer. The reason or, more accurately, pretext for this demand was the unification of two sections into a single division, but the real motivation was the desire of management to satisfy the mid-level managers by promotion. My opinion was that adding another managerial layer would be a fatal error that would be rued for years to come; it would also exacerbate the managerial obsession with status. I tried persuading the CEO and the senior managers that it was unwise, and I obviously proposed a model that would allow the

Space for comments & insight

unification of the sections without adding another level of management. I explained that all leading organizations in the world and all organizational approaches tend towards flattening organizational hierarchies. I warned that extending the communications chain would damage the organization's flexibility and functioning; I showed how the scope of accountability at every organizational level would shrink as the result of adding a managerial layer and create an unjustified opening for demands for salary increases in order to compensate those who would not be promoted in the move. The struggle was extraordinarily difficult, but in the end the CEO was convinced and the move was blocked. I was very unpopular with management; even my own team did not believe I would succeed in preventing the addition of the new managerial layer. I felt like Don Quixote fighting the windmills, but I honestly believed I was giving the best service possible to that nebulous entity called "the good of the organization." I could, of course, have chosen a more convenient way. Had I supported the suggestion and carried it out as part of my duties as the company's VP of HR, I would have accrued power, expanded my authority, and managed a large-scope project that would have given me many bonus points. No one would have accused me of irresponsibility. The results, which according to my belief would have been bad for the organization, would have come to light only years later and would not have been placed at my doorstep but rather at the CEO's. But in my own view I would have failed in my job. In this case, the goal I chose as part of responsibility as VP of HR was to keep the organization effective and flat and resist the understandable but harmful human tendencies and needs.

From discussing the goals of the space, we shall now make the transition to discussing its boundaries.

Space for comments & insight

The Boundaries of Space

In order to avoid chaotic conduct, space must be anchored in the earthly, concrete world of physical, social and value-based boundaries. The writer and philosopher A.S. Neill, the spiritual father and founder of the Summerhill School in Leiston, Suffolk, believed that children should be educated through giving them freedom. He embarked on an experiential and philosophical journey that went through three stations in his lifetime. As the result of this journey, he wrote *Summerhill: A Radical Approach to Child Rearing*, *Talking of Summerhill* and *Freedom, Not License!* (I became familiar with these books as a teen because all three were published in Hebrew by the eponymous publishing house of my late grandfather, Yehoshua Chechik, in the 1960s). In the third of these books, Neill claims that freedom exists within boundaries; without boundaries, there is no freedom, only license.

Managing boundaries is, I think, one of the most important issues in management in general and the second most important parameter in the management of space. From my own experience, I can say that when a system is not functioning properly, one should seek the source of the problem first in goal articulation and afterwards in the presence and clarity of the boundaries. When boundaries are given and held, our ability to handle difficulties and confront challenges rises immensely compared to a situation in which the boundaries are unknown or weak.

I have participated in a number of workshops given by HOSHEV–Research of Social Innovations and Changes and Ofek – the Israeli association of studding groups and organization, two associations in Israel that implement the psychoanalytical systemic approach, an outgrowth of the Tavistock

Space for comments & insight

Institute in London. The approach deals with organizational dynamics and subconscious processes. A workshop usually lasts a week, and is strict with time and territorial boundaries that are very well defined and rigid. Workshop managers start the activity at precise the pre-set time and without regard for the number of participants in the room or whatever else is happening in it, and conclude at precisely the set time, also regardless of what is happening, even if it means cutting off a participant in mid-sentence. Throughout the workshop there was a complete separation between workshop leaders and participants. The former ate at a separate table and made sure that they were not overheard by the latter. This conduct arouses anger and puzzlement on the part of the participant attending the workshop for the first time. At the same time, they internalize the boundaries right away. The process of the workshop's work is designed to arouse anxiety and touch the subconscious, but the existence of a set of very firm boundaries of time and place serves as a holding and containing element for workshop participants. Obviously, in a company that is not a weeklong workshop but may have hundreds or tens of thousands of employees, setting boundaries and managing them is much more complex.

Every organizational space has several types of boundaries:

Physical boundaries:

Among the physical boundaries we may notes budgets, manpower, the physical installation of the unit, and the geographical boundaries of the region in which it operates. These boundaries are the simplest and the easiest for the organization to maintain: - the chances that a unit manager will come to work on a random Tuesday morning and walk into the office of a different unit manager and sit down in his or her seat are slim. When the expenditures of a unit officeholder exceed the budget set for him/her, it is reasonable to assume

Space for comments & insight

that the budget & control unit of the organization's finance section will have something to say. Should the sales manager of the northern district initiate a sales project in the central district, it will be clear to everyone that s/he has overstepped the boundaries. Therefore, these boundaries are relatively simple to manage and are in most organizations fairly well managed. Therefore I shall not expand any further.

Professional boundaries:

Professional boundaries are at times simple and easy to define, and at times less so. The more the officeholder's profession requires more specialized knowledge, so the boundary will be clearer. Neurosurgery, nuclear physics, electronics and chemistry have clearer and more easily defined – and maintained – boundaries than the professional boundaries of marketing and human resources. Nonetheless, organizations sometimes invite – justifiably and cleverly – the mixing of professional boundaries, such as between R&D and marketing, or between psychology and medicine. As the complexity of the task rises and the areas within it are closer, there may be a confusion of boundaries. For example, in the process of developing a new product, the product will be marketed through cooperation between two spaces in the organization. In the new space – the joint space or the intersection between the two spaces – the engineer in charge of the product's development and the marketing director in charge of marketing the finished product will both operate. These officeholders may find themselves investing a lot of energy into clarifying the boundaries with regard to the demands of this product, the target audience and the marketing methods. Each one will act by entering the space of the other; when this happens, interpersonal and organizational tensions surface.

The more senior the position and the more complex the task, the larger component of responsibility will be and the greater the potential for blurring

Space for comments & insight

the boundaries. Conflicts between R&D personnel and the marketing branches of companies are hardly uncommon - Such tension is inevitable and perhaps even a good thing. It may be viewed either as an organizational failure or as an opportunity. Improper management of boundaries and the organizational tension that is created in such situations may create two problematic patterns of conduct. The first, and more dire, is the regressive pattern of managers who interface at the boundary. Each operates only at the level of accountability to avoid friction, as if saying, "It's not for me to argue." This approach leaves areas between the two spaces unattended. The second pattern is the struggle for power and territory that steals a lot of energy and creates conflict without any value accruing to the company. However, the proper construction of and intermediate space between development and marketing and the proper management of this temporary space may create a value that did not exist before and allow the participants in the space to contribute of their human capital and generate better results.

In the period during which I managed HR at the 'yes' Satellite TV Company, there was a permanent situation of blurred boundaries between the sales unit and the service unit. Sales reps would complete the sales process with a new customer and transfer the sales agreement with customer data to the service unit in order to connect the customer to the company's TV service. Seemingly, at this point, the accountability of the sales rep ended and that of the service branch began, to handle the installation of the infrastructure at the customer's home. However, if, as the result of faulty functioning of the service section, the customer would seek to revoke the decision to connect to 'yes' – something that would happen from time to time – the sales rep would lose out on the sales bonus. The company's working processes created this interim space, but it was not managed as such. Instead of, a priori, defining this space as a joint space of sales and service in which the sales rep and the service rep were both

Space for comments & insight

accountable for the complete conclusion of the task, this interim space became a space for conflicts. Incorrect definition and improper management of the space cost the company more than a few customers and sales reps their bonuses. When the company understood that the loss of customers stemmed from the improper management of the spaces, it established a designated service hotline that worked with sales reps throughout the process of connecting the new customers. This process generated direct relationships between the rep doing the selling and the rep handling service, both working to connect the new customer to the satellite service. This action created a joint space for the sales reps and service reps, which led to a significant reduction in the loss of customers than had been the case in the customers' transition from the sales space to the service space.

Boundaries of time:

Time boundaries are usually easy to identify in an organization's routine. Meetings are set for a pre-arranged hour, projects and tasks have deadlines, and even the number of hours one spends at work is determined ahead of time. Nevertheless, not everything that is easily identified is also easily realized. In practice, in many organizations the boundaries of time are not respected and certainly are not accorded the respect they deserve. The boundaries of time are also the boundaries of the space itself, not just boundaries within it. When we determine the goal of the organization, it lacks meaning unless time is also considered. When we construct a vision for an organization without the boundaries of time, it is no different from a dream. Moreover, in the dynamic model we are discussing, the ticking of time is the most critical boundary of all. The validity of goals, like the validity of the boundaries, changes given circumstances and time. The boundaries of time of goals may lose their validity without us noticing. When the validity expires, they cease to fulfill

Space for comments & insight

their important function and might even steer the organization's activity in a direction that is no longer relevant. I shall expand on the boundaries of time in the chapter dealing with the issue of vision within the realm of space management.

The boundaries of the job and the boundaries of impact, or the boundaries of accountability and the boundaries of responsibility:

The difference between accountability and responsibility has been defined in Chapter 1. The boundaries of accountability are usually defined ahead of time by the organization in an operative manner. The VP of HR must provide a response to the need for recruitment and training. S/he handles company events, disciplinary infractions, organizational surveys, organizational development, and so on. Should s/he decide to handle the raising of funds, s/he would have exceeded his/her function at the level of accountability. In contrast to these boundaries, which are relatively clear and fairly simply managed, the boundaries of responsibility are more complex. These are affected by the employee's internal layers and are not always identifiable ahead of time or manageable. These are the boundaries within which the individual operates and affects the environment relevant to him/her in the organization. In order to demonstrate the complexity of defining boundaries in the realm of responsibility, I shall use an example from my first job as the head of a team in the Youth Development Department at the Tel Aviv Municipality. I was responsible for several south Tel Aviv neighborhoods. Our tasks were clear. We were to interact with teens who had dropped out of school and gotten caught up in life on the streets. The goal was to bring them back to any sort of educational setting or to steer them towards gainful employment. My first two years in the job were extremely difficult and

Space for comments & insight

frustrating, and my measure of success extremely low. The good that came out of it was minimal, despite the fact we did everything we were supposed to, and more. Because of the great and growing frustration within the team and the tendency of employees to leave, I was required to put in more resources into keeping them instead of investing all of my energy into the youths. After two years of frustration, I took a look at the boundaries that defined the target group we were dealing with. The boundaries formulated obligated us to deal with teens who had already dropped out of school, a target group with which the chances for success given our resources were very low. I assumed the responsibility and redefined the target group as being youths at risk of dropping out of school. From that point onwards, we invested most of our efforts into that group. The decision was extremely difficult because it meant not working with the disengaged teens in those neighborhoods that entire year. The moral dilemma was clear, as was the fact that we had exceeded the mandate given to us. However, it was clear to me that without moving the boundaries that defined the target group, we would continue in vain to try to save kids from drugs and crime whose chances were slim while no one would be trying to prevent other kids from following the same trajectory. That year we had great success. Many youths, who had been at risk for dropping out, were treated and remained in their schools, and the total number of kids disengaged from the school system that year was lower. One could say that the change in defining the boundaries of the task allowed us to meet the goal better. This is the nature of responsibility. Unlike accountability, its boundaries are flexible and errors in it are borne by the officeholder. On the other hand operating in the circle of responsibility allows many times a real breakthrough.

The function of the boundaries of space is to allow officeholders to fulfill

Space for comments & insight

their capabilities and insights within the circle of responsibility. When the boundaries of a space are too rigid and do not allow for freedom or, alternately, are chaotic and fail to maintain order and organization, there will be no expression of activity in the circle of responsibility. Moreover, since all organizations operate in an environment lacking resources (even if artificially so), there is a constant pull to operate in the circle of accountability; thus, there is no space left for acting in the realm of responsibility. Therefore, the manger of space must construct and manage the boundaries of the space such that they allow the actualization of responsibility by the personnel in that space. Of course, the more senior the officeholder and the greater his/her capabilities, the greater the circle of responsibility is compared to the circle of accountability; the more junior the officeholder, so the circle of responsibility will be smaller than the circle of accountability.

A hierarchy and organizational structure divide an organization into levels of activity. The closer the unit's task is to the customer, so the measure of immediate, daily accountability grows at the expense of long-term responsibility. The farther the unit is from the customer, so the immediate, daily accountability shrinks while the responsibility grows. A bank teller who provides service for customers waiting in line provides the immediate response at the level of accountability to the bank's customers. This teller has limited resources of time or thought to conceive of initiatives and activities in the realm of responsibility, such as changing work procedures designed to shorten lines. By contrast, it would be right and proper that the department manager be more available to deal with issues within the realm of responsibility, such as reducing waiting time of customers. The branch manager should occupy himself only with issues in the realm of responsibility such as work procedures, the positioning of the branch, its

Space for comments & insight

profitability and the profitability of the bank. The right thing to do would be to create a structure within every organizational unit that has a clear nucleus of tasks and products at the level of organizational accountability together with room for making an impact. When the nucleus of accountability of an organizational unit does not receive sufficient response, the entire structure sinks in order to provide the right level of responses to the organization's requirements at the level of accountability. However, when the level of accountability receives a response, the entire structure rises to the level of responsibility. If we again turn to the example of the bank, if the tellers are unable to provide an appropriate response to customers waiting in line, we would expect the department manager, and perhaps even the branch manager, to step in and act. Nonetheless, we also expect that after they finish dealing with the problem, it would be the department manager and the branch manager who would look for solutions that would prevent the problematic situation from arising again. In order to describe this part of constructing boundaries as part of the architecture of space, I have chosen to use the floatation device principle. I have chosen this term because the floatation device— in our case representing responsibility – creates constant opposition to the weight of the load – representing accountability – pulling the floatation device down, against its nature. This means that an organizational structure must be constructed in such a way as to maintain constantly the resources and activities in the realm of responsibility and not give in and sink into activity in the realm of accountability alone.

When the operational units provide a full response at the level of accountability, the other layers are free to fulfill their responsibility. When the operational layer or the level of accountability fails to meet their tasks, all

Space for comments & insight

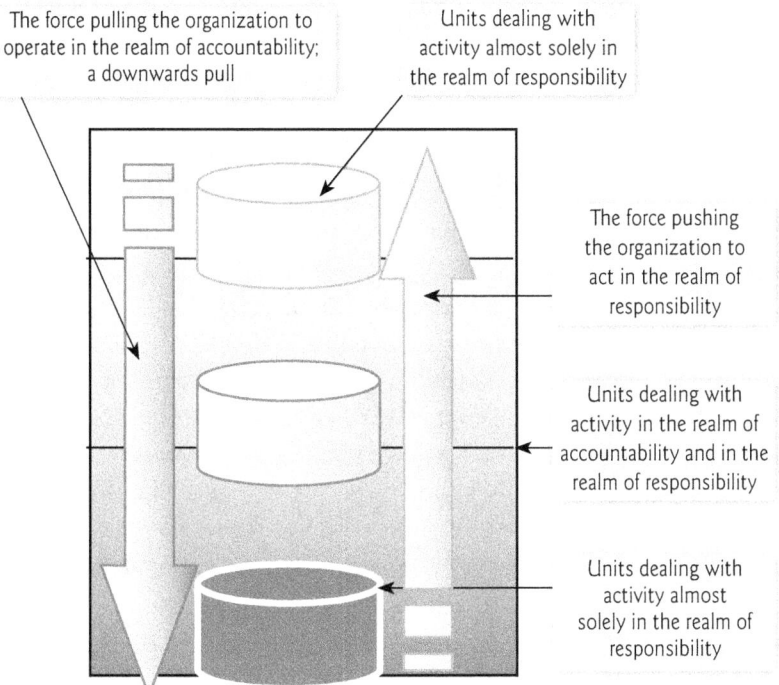

The floatation device principle

the other layers will sink to accountability tasks. This means that spaces will shrink and energy will be invested into accountability. By contrast, when the response to the demands of accountability is sufficient, resources are freed up to operate in the realm of responsibility. Then, even employees whose daily operation is only at the level of accountability may take responsibility and attempt to influence their environment.

Space for comments & insight

Managers in organizations who are required to reduce expenditures and so decide to terminate employees sometimes make the mistake of firing those whose ability to bear responsibility is greater, because they tend to earn more money, leaving behind those who operate only in the realm of accountability. When the organization gets back on its feet, the employees left are either inexperienced or incapable of bearing responsibility and lack the human capital capable of restoring the organization to the state it was in before the crisis. By contrast, proper management of cutbacks leaves the right proportion of potential, both in the realm of accountability and in the realm of responsibility, and allows the organization to return to its previous scope of activity. At the end of 2000 and beginning of 2001, Soda Club Group, was forced to go through significant downsizing because of competition that caused a decrease of about 50% of its sales turnover. In the process of cutting back, we made sure to preserve skilled key people, despite the fact that their salaries were higher. We believed that the crisis was temporary and we knew that if we gave up these employees, it would take us a long time to return to the level of capabilities that were part of the company's human capital. The step proved itself, and a year later the company returned to its pattern of rapid growth.

Value-laden boundaries:

Of all the possible organizational boundaries, there is one type that requires particular attention – the moral/value-laden boundaries of the space. Goals and a vision indicate the place we want to reach, whereas values shape the roads we take to get there. Values, whatever they are, are the most important component in the existence of a space. For someone to make his or her way in the organizational space, s/he must be familiar with its norms of conduct. An organization in which there are no value-laden boundaries and in which

Space for comments & insight

any behavior is legitimate in order to attain the goals defines, in practice, the goals as the sole value. An organization that ignores the fact that its employees are transgressing the law, lie to one another and to customers, and undermine the work of colleagues in order to promote themselves in competition over status and success in the organization, defines a set of values according to which the personal place and personal success stand at the center. It is necessary to understand that values need not be always positive, and therefore negative values can make set of value-laden boundries as well. Many organizations support negative values and it would be a serious error not to call these by name. The existence of negative values is not the same as a lack of values: we see the existence of the strongest codes of values in criminal organizations, where the punishment for transgression is severe and immediate. I don't want to sound naïve or more pious than anyone else, but I am convinced that the lack of boundaries of the startups and financial institutions – especially value-laden ones – was the reason for the high-tech bubble bursting ten years ago and the current financial and real estate crisis. Absent value-laden boundaries, when the only goal of management and employees is immediate profits and enormous bonuses, everything breaks apart. When the bottom line of the next quarter becomes the exclusive goal of an organization and the bonus is the manager's only goal, everything else loses meaning and the organization is left without any real anchors. When I speak of values and boundaries, I do not mean to say that social benefit must be placed ahead of commercial benefit, but to link the two together. Organizations that lose their value-laden boundaries do not necessarily come out ahead in the long run.

In each of the three companies where I headed HR, the system of value was forced to confront difficulties in how to conduct themselves with regard to employees who were stricken by cancer, something that unfortunately

Space for comments & insight

happened more than once. In one of the companies several employees fell ill with cancer during my tenure there; they all received full company support. No question was raised regarding paying their salaries even after their sick days were used up. The HR department supported them morally and financially throughout the period they were fighting the disease. By contrast, at another one of the companies I worked there were questions about how to deal with the lack of sick days. When one of the HR managers came to me with her uncertainty about an employee who'd become ill, I immediately drew the value-laden boundaries by saying that the number of sick days to which the employee was entitled or how long we had to keep paying her salary, regardless of the labor law, was of no concern to us, because we would continue to pay it in full. Furthermore, when it became clear that she needed treatment not covered by her health plan, the company donated tens of thousands of shekels to pay for it. The employee recovered and came back to work for the company for many more years. When another employee fell ill, the rules were already in place. Unfortunately, this employee did not beat the disease and passed away, but the company continued to care for his family members until they were back on their feet. In another company where I headed HR, an employee was diagnosed with cancer. When his sick days were used up, HR personnel terminated his job with the company. He ended his life without any support from or connection with the company. I found out about his illness when I received an email about the funeral. Without a doubt, the failure lay in the company's value system in general, and with the HR manager in that division in particular; of course, the failure as a whole was my responsibility. The differences in the way each of the three companies dealt with similar situations were a direct result of the differences between their organizational values. In the first company, how to behave was obvious and no questions needed to be asked; in the second, questions were raised; in the third, there were again no questions but for reasons that differed greatly from the first. The greater the

Space for comments & insight

gap between the organization's values in practice and the values it seeks to instill, the more difficult the process of instilling them will be.

While the example above relates to rather rare, though important, occurrences in the life of a company and would seem to have had no implication for the company's commercial success, values are critical for the success of a company no matter what its field of endeavor, and value-laden boundaries are of utmost significance. Without them, it is difficult to maintain the other boundaries. The current financial crisis is replete with examples that make it painfully clear that the crisis is the result of companies that acted without value-laden boundaries, and lacking these there were no boundaries whatsoever. Instead of freedom of action within boundaries there was license, characterized by the fact that many of the most senior officeholders, responsible for the global economy, operated only on the basis of personal interests and steered the world into a crisis.

The boundaries of the space are critical parameters in the employees' understanding of what is expected of them, the freedom they have to operate, develop as people, and to make an impact. Employees will try to challenge the boundaries. In fact, I wish for every organization that its employees and managers do so. However, the existence of boundaries, if they are clear and rational and linked to both business and social values, gives people a sense of confidence, meaning, and the desire to grow as individuals, and, finally, represents a great contribution to the organization. When the boundaries are unclear, irrational and dissociated from business and social values, an organization will experience confusion, lack of confidence, and a sense of helplessness; these will be reflected in a reduction of activity, a refusal to assume responsibility, as well as the curbing of personal development and minimal contribution to the organization.

Space for comments & insight

There is no need for a multitude of rules and regulations attending to every last matter in an organization. Too many boundaries can also create lack of clarity and confusion. The sales managers at 'yes' were asked to articulate the boundaries of behavior for the field sales organization. At the beginning of the process, some fifteen boundaries were proposed, from boundaries regarding appearance to boundaries regarding deadlines. In order to clarify the influence of so many boundaries on the team functioning, I used a metaphor: "This room," I said, "has four walls. That is a convenient space for the purpose of our work. Of course, we could have had this discussion on the lawn, but we all remember when we were in high school, how "effective" the classes held on the lawn in good weather were. The parallel to that is having no boundaries. By contrast, this room could have been constructed out of fifteen walls. I have a hard time seeing how we'd be able to do our work in a space that resembled a maze more than a room. This means that a relatively small number of boundaries to contain the space are important. Moreover," I added, "a boundary is a boundary. Once you've decided to draw it, you have to be sure you don't intend to cross it and that it is not dependent on circumstances." In the ongoing processing and thinking, the team examined all the boundaries suggested. Some were consolidated into a simpler and more general statement. Regarding others, the team agreed they were insufficiently important to serve as boundaries. By the end of the process, the team selected three boundaries of conduct: meetings sales goals (after all, it was a sales organization and without sales it would cease to be), human dignity, and honesty in every situation.

The measure of flexibility of boundaries changes depending on the type of space and according to the organizational and business environment, the content area in which the organization operates and the nature of its managers. In space management, the space is more effective when the boundaries are few and transparency high.

Space for comments & insight

Degrees of Freedom in the Space

Degrees of freedom concern the management of freedom within the boundaries of the space as a function of constraints, such as the organization's situation, the business and social environment in which it operates, and the personal abilities of the people operating in the space. At times senior managers will reduce or expand the levels of freedom of their subordinates, while at other times degrees of freedom are self-regulated, i.e., managers or employees will reduce or expand their own degrees of freedom according to their own assessment of the need in coordination and approval of their superiors. Real freedom, freedom that is not anarchy or license, is always proportional; therefore, I shall use the phrase "degrees of freedom."

Where people manage their own space and operate independently, they experience freedom and respond with great involvement in every aspect of their activity – conduct, emotion, motivation, accountability, and responsibility.

The first example of different degrees of freedom I would like to give is not taken from the world of employment, but it does clarify what I mean by degrees of freedom and the connection between them and the level of personal involvement expressed in the space.

When we were in school, we encountered several types of examinations:

- Multiple-choice exams
- Many short open-ended questions
- A few general and inclusive open-ended questions
- A project on a topic chosen from the curriculum (e.g., a seminar paper)

Space for comments & insight

These four types of examinations reflect the degree of freedom of the examinee. Students may express more comprehensive and varied knowledge, their ability to formulate and explain and their creativity, stances and independent thinking, the larger the space is. Multiple-choice tests limit the examinee to selecting the correct answers. There is no room for explaining, deliberating, or even saying that none of the answers is correct (unless there is a choice that reads, "None of the above"). In this type of examination, the degrees of freedom are so constrained as to allow us to say that there is no space whatsoever.

An examination composed of short answer questions usually tests simple knowledge and also does not require a great deal of involvement on the examinees' part, although a little more than a multiple-choice test. Thus, space exists but to a limited extent.

An open-ended examination composed of questions that require that the examinees integrate the material, construct theses and prove them, and perhaps even present a personal position, creates an additional degree of freedom and, respectively, greater space for examinees to invest more and demonstrate greater involvement.

In a seminar paper, Master's thesis or doctorate, the degree of freedom is the highest because it allows the learners to choose the topic they are going to write about, construct a thesis, present a position, draw conclusions, make ethical and moral claims, and propose new perspectives. Thus, this type of examination offers a great deal of space.

The extent of the examination's effect on the learners' involvement grows as the degrees of freedom expand. As proof, I offer the fact that no one

Space for comments & insight

remembers the examinations s/he took, many remember seminar papers, and no one ever forgets his or her Master's thesis or doctorate.

I shall give another example of the different degrees of freedom in a space. Two hundred people are invited to a lecture hall for two hours. They arrive to find the chairs stacked in the corners, the dais on castors so that it can be moved, and around the hall tables with arts and crafts supplies. No one is there to issue any instructions. Those in attendance have a space with degrees of freedom determined by the opportunities the hall presents – chairs, arts and crafts materials, a sound system and CDs, and two hours of time. They are free to set goals for themselves, either as individuals or a group, or not set any goals at all. Whoever wants to can take a chair and sit down to watch and wait for someone else to tell him or her what to do. Others can take arts and crafts supplies and draw or sculpt, while others can put on music and start to dance. The space is totally chaotic and therefore I can pretty well assume that most people will go to the cafeteria for a cup of coffee. Very few will take advantage of the opportunity to create something. On the other hand, were the lecture that was planned actually to take place, those invited would have very few degrees of freedom, namely to show up or not and to listen to the lecture or not.

I have presented two extremes, one chaotic and the other closed. There are of course interim situations. Let us assume that the goal of the space is to allow people to learn, experientially, the effective management of space. It is possible to determine time frame for working in groups or in plenary sessions, to define authority and processes, and to define a team to consult for the process. Under such circumstances participants would experience their own difficulties in dealing with a situation in which there are no boundaries and there are no agreed-upon, organized processes, compared to the sense of

Space for comments & insight

relief that would ensue when they start to create some boundaries and it becomes possible to plan and coordinate action.

We can say that as boundaries increase and degrees of freedom decrease, so the space shrinks. As boundaries decrease and degrees of freedom increase, so the space expands. The connection between the parameters of space is what creates the size of the space and its impact.

Managing space according to the model presented in this book is dynamic and requires matching the space to the organization's needs and the people operating in it. When the goal presented to the people operating in the space is focused and short term, e.g., organizational change, the space is smaller and its boundaries more numerous and rigid; such a situation may even require close supervision of the quality of the products and schedules. By contrast, a distant and more general goal, such as constructing a long-term strategic plan, allows a larger space, i.e., fewer boundaries and more degrees of freedom. Nonetheless, I shall make a general claim: in every situation it is possible and right to grant more space and a greater extent of freedom than those we might be inclined towards.

Managing Degrees of Freedom

People differ in their need for space in which to act and their extent of freedom of action. Some need a great deal of freedom, to the point that they are unable to belong to an organization unless they are the entrepreneurs and even then, once the organization is established, they are constantly shaking the boundaries and unsettling its routine. Soda Club Ltd. was managed by an entrepreneur who needed so much personal freedom that decisions made in

Space for comments & insight

a meeting he ran just before flying abroad would be radically altered before he landed at his destination. This type of entrepreneur is well described by Prof. Ichak Adizes in his book *How to Solve the Mismanagement Crisis*, which he calls "the fire starter," i.e., an entrepreneur who, as long as the organization is orderly, tries to overturn it.

Unlike the entrepreneur, some people have an almost nonexistent need for degrees of freedom. Such people cling to jobs in which there is a great deal of routine (an accounting clerk who balances the books or production line workers who spend decades next to the same machine and are unwilling to try a different position). At Dead Sea Periclase, I knew one of the line operators who had worked for fifteen years in exactly the same spot, a simple, uneducated man, who had developed a great deal of expertise in his particular position. No attempt to train him on another machine succeeded. The least amount of uncertainty made him anxious.

Naturally, those who need more space can also handle what it demands: independence, the ability to handle uncertainty and anxiety, the ability to assume responsibility and to make decisions, and the willingness to bear the results of errors. These will be promoted to more senior positions than those whose space threaten them and prefer fewer degrees of freedom. To the same extent that different employees need different degrees of freedom, so different managers are capable of allowing different degrees of freedom, and those who need space do not necessarily know how to give it to others.

A basic rule in space management says that boundaries and degrees of freedom must be clear both to the manager and the employee. This means that both the organization and the managers are willing to take the risk that the employee will not meet the task fully or even partially and they

Space for comments & insight

will nevertheless not intrude into the employee's space. Of course, should the employee fail to deliver the goods, it would be perfectly legitimate not to employ him or her for long. In such a case one could say the space was too big for the employee. Nevertheless, when an officeholder does not have enough degrees of freedom in the space, s/he loses the sense of ownership and responsibility for the space and the space is not space anymore.

While the goals and boundaries are identical parameters for all the people operating in the space, the degrees of freedom are a parameter that may differ from one person to another, according to their abilities and needs. Therefore, managers' familiarity with the needs of their personnel and their ability to handle freedom is of critical importance. I have mentioned a number of times that this philosophy of management is a developmental one and deals with the development of the space. Almost anyone can learn to live with an expanding measure of freedom. When my daughters were three and six, I put a lot of time into building them a clothes closet. After I was done, all that was left was to choose the handles for the doors and drawers. At that point, my spouse and I decided that we would let our older, six-year old daughter do the choosing. Of course, we asked ourselves what we would do were she to choose "little-girl" handles, and we decided that in the worst case scenario the closet would have inappropriate handles but we wouldn't veto her choice. The closet is still standing. It is now more than 20 years old and still has the handles my daughter chose, handles that turned out to be very suitable indeed. Everyone, at every age and in every situation, can learn to live with a growing amount of freedom. A manager's ability to identify the place the employee is at and guide him or her through the process of learning towards greater independence as manager and employee will constantly develop and expand the human capital available to the organization and the employee's contribution to the space.

Space for comments & insight

When I began working as the head of HR at Soda Club Ltd., a very skilled and experienced payroll accountant in the finance section was in charge of salaries. He was meticulous, precise and very careful. The problem was that the payroll system was handled almost entirely by hand. Soda Club was about to triple its workforce; it was necessary to computerize the payroll system. As the number of employees increased, it was necessary to add manpower to payroll, so it was decided to take on a payroll clerk in HR. The payroll accountant, despite being an excellent professional, was very conservative in his approach and made it difficult to develop the system. I therefore decided to take advantage of the new position of payroll clerk in order to train the accountant's replacement.

At the same time, we recruited a temp named Etti to a different position. She was an experienced accountant who had worked at a different company and I was impressed by her professionalism and personality. After a number of weeks, during which I had made a point of paying attention to her work, it occurred to me that she was an excellent candidate for the job of Soda Club's next payroll accountant. At that point I told Etti what I had in mind for her and that I expected that she would assume more payroll tasks so she could learn all that was necessary to serve as the company's payroll accountant. But after about six months I saw that nothing was moving. I invited her into my office and I tried to understand where she was stuck. Etti, a woman of principles and morals, was very ill at ease with the idea that she, by her activity and growth, was going to be displacing another employee. I explained to her that it would happen with or without her, that I believed in her and would be very happy for her to have the job. However, should she decide that she didn't want it, I would of course respect her choice. I asked her to let me know her decision after the weekend. After the weekend, she told me she wanted the job after all. I asked her what I could do to help her, and she pointed out a number of

Space for comments & insight

topics in which she felt she needed more training; I approved her requests. At the same time, it was clear to me that the main thing I could do for her was to steer her in the direction of growing independence in her work. The process lasted several months, after which she was appointed payroll accountant for the company. Even in that position, I encouraged her to greater independence, which she assumed in full. Beyond her routine accountability, she also operated a great deal in the circle of responsibility. She initiated changes, identified flaws in the reporting system and irregularities with regard to norms and labor laws and regulations. She initiated the development of the salary system and became an important address for all of the company's managers and employees as she always gave excellent service as well as accurate, quick and comprehensive reporting and advice. She issued reports she had initiated and helped to build management tools that contributed to many managers; this was certainly true of me. Etti never stayed in her comfort zone; she never avoided speaking out or using her discretion. Chances are that this woman would have remained an excellent clerk all her working life had no one given her the space to grow that would lead her to grow into a greater amount of freedom, leading to functioning and action that allowed her to actualize the human capital within her. This is a simple example. The real difficulty lies in giving space to people who are likely to operate within the boundaries of the space against your wishes or preferences. This is the constant dilemma of the manager of space, one that I have encountered countless times in my life, and it concerns the balance between providing freedom and independence to your personnel to act, create and have an impact using the best human capital within them, and maintaining the direction, quality of performance, and primarily the boundaries and values.

As a manager, I learned very quickly that if I desire my people to do exactly what I think they ought to do, I will find myself constantly telling them what

Space for comments & insight

to do. To my mind, such work is tedious and boring and does not leave me the space I need to perform my own tasks. Therefore, in order to create the value I believed I could bring to the organization, I had to erect a framework of goals and boundaries that would allow my people the freedom to act, even should they choose actions that were not always to my liking. Many managers worked in spaces I managed. None of them was easy and every one of them was constantly challenging everything, but they operated on the basis of their understanding within the boundaries I had set up. At times they would come to me for authorization for actions they knew I wouldn't like and would wear me down with their arguments. It was clear to them and to me that, at any time, I could have made the decision and not allowed them to do what they thought was right. But I avoided doing so because I knew that that would make me into the responsible party and I wanted them to bear the responsibility. Let them lose sleep over it! Finally, the value brought by this freedom I allowed them was inestimably greater than the cost of the few mishaps that occurred. There may even have been more mishaps had I been in charge of it all.

To this point we have dealt with the structural architecture of space constructed of goals, boundaries and degrees of freedom. Before going on to the psychological and social architecture of space, I want to devote some thought to the question of the frequency of assessing these structural components.

The Dynamics of Space and Spiral Management

Western culture in general and management culture in particular is constructed on linear, result-oriented thought, while the space management approach is constructed on spiral thought. I began this book by saying that

---

Space for comments & insight

the world is changing at a speed that does not allow us to leave the same product on the shelf for long. This is also true of management products. Companies define a vision and it usually remains in place for far too long. Not only do companies fail to go back and redefine it, they also relate to it as sacrosanct. The true life span of management products is short and in the absence of an updated product people, who operate in the space, are operating with tools whose validity has expired or without any tools at all. When we are required to validate and update management products we see that each one has a different life expectancy.

Visions and goals naturally have the longest life span. They are the foundation on which the organization was established and the reason for its existence. By contrast, boundaries change all the time. Geographical boundaries change into professional boundaries. A customer service call in the United States will receive a response in excellent English from India. The order placement center of a direct marketing company in the Netherlands will answer and deal with the sale and delivery of an espresso machine in Switzerland. Changes in value-laden boundaries and norms of behavior also change and require constant assessment as the result of commercial activity in a global economy.

However, the parameter with the shortest life span is the degrees of freedom. The rapidly changing economic situation, market conditions and business environment require the constant management of boundaries and degrees of freedom. At times of growth and fight for market shares, space should be expanded, but when the struggle is for profitability or in times of crisis and tight competition, space should be contracted, e.g., reducing the scope of resources, moving them at the right time in favor of one space at the expense of another, reducing and at times even canceling degrees of freedom in order to make it through a crisis. However, when the reason for reducing the

Space for comments & insight

degrees of freedom passes, it is necessary to rebuild the spaces and restore the degrees of freedom. Consequently, we find that today a key management task is to manage the changes in spaces and adapt them to a changing reality, to reexamine and update the definitions of goals and the vision, to redefine of boundaries, and constantly to construct degrees of freedom. Furthermore, even if the commercial environment does not change, our perspective does. Passing time and personal and professional development affect the way we view reality. What once seemed true doesn't anymore. Therefore the validity of each one of the structural parameters we have created for the space must also be adapted. Spiral thinking requires constant and relatively frequent examination of each one of the parameters suggested.

Until now we have deal with the mechanical qualities of space without which it does not exist. From here on we will be dealing with the manager's function in managing the social and psychological qualities of the space.

Space for comments & insight

The Social Psychological Architecture of Space: Holding and Containing

The structural components of space – the goals, boundaries and degrees of freedom – are the elements without which there is no space. However, they are necessary but not sufficient for effective space management. I have already noted elsewhere that real freedom, even when existing within boundaries, induces anxiety. Organizations in general, and commercial ones in particular, have to confront the existential anxiety of the organization as well as the personal anxieties of workers and managers. The nature of anxiety is that it shrinks space because it generates more boundaries even when these are unnecessary and limits degrees of freedom even where it is possible to grant a great deal of freedom. Therefore, in addition to the structural elements of space we must also sustain two social psychological processes in it.

Holding and Containing in Space Management

The social and psychological atmosphere to a great degree affects the extent to which the potential of the human capital in a given space is going to be realized. In order to construct effectiveness in the space, the atmosphere in it must be expressed in two central psychological and social processes

Space for comments & insight

– holding and containing. These are important elements in every authority: parents, teachers, army commanders, and managers, of course, serve both to hold and maintain the boundaries and goals and to contain and process emotions in general and anxieties in particular. When holding and containing are imbalanced the result is an imbalanced space.

Authority figures who focus only on holding the boundaries and goals and neglect to contain and process the range of emotions in the space, including those of the people in their authority and under their responsibility, will damage their subordinates' capacity for satisfaction even if they are fulfilling their tasks. By contrast, authority figures who contain and process the gamut of emotions and anxieties in the space but fail to hold the boundaries and maintain the goals damage the ability to the people operating in the space to fulfill the goals of the space. And authority figures who neither hold the boundaries nor contain anxieties leave the space abandoned both emotionally and functionally.

Holding in Management

Goals, boundaries and degrees of freedom require the existence of a stable, constant nucleus. Goals that change frequently without explanation, the lack of a clear connection between the goals, the decisions being made and the conduct of the organization, boundaries that are either unclear or not respected, and, of course, degrees of freedom that change without logical reasons, do not create an experience of space but rather of chaos and confusion. This confusion may be experienced as a loss of direction and create a space that is unpredictable. Such a space will lack a sense of confidence, and decision-making at every level of the organization will be difficult. This will result in organizational anxiety or functional indifference

Space for comments & insight

and lead to ineffectiveness that, in extreme cases, can be actual paralysis. Therefore, holding goals, boundaries and degrees of freedom is very important. Nevertheless, we must beware of confusing holding with rigidity. The parameters, when held properly, are both flexible and consistent, and it is possible to doubt, raise questions and discuss them, while at the same time it is impossible to dismiss or ignore them. Just as the space manager must deal with them so the subordinates may examine them.

The more challenging the goals of the space are, the more there will be pieces that will be hard to accept and internalize. This does not mean it is necessary to simplify them, but it is necessary to take into account that they will generate doubt about the possibility of realizing them and that a lot of work with the organization will be necessary in order to process them into something understandable and clear. The clearer the parameters of the space are, the easier it is for the managers of the secondary spaces to identify with them and operate within them. The organization's handling of them will be simple and comfortable and their holding will be easy. The more complex the parameters are, the harder to grasp and understand, the more difficult it will be for managers of the secondary spaces to internalize them and identify and agree with them. The managers will find it hard to operate on their basis and a great deal of organizational energy will be invested in processing and holding them, finally requiring much more managerial investment.

Holding in space has two functions: one is maintaining the assets of the space, i.e., goals, boundaries and degrees of freedom, and the other is creating a psychological and social organizational environment that is consistent and stable despite the fluctuations and changes that are a part of any organization. The components of space become its identity. The more consistent this identity is, the more the organization's personnel will internalize it and the

Space for comments & insight

more it will become an intuitive guiding principle. This may be compared to a person who views himself as generous, good-hearted and honest and who considers these traits to be his personality. This identity of the self will serve as the yardstick for every action he takes. Actions that do not match this identity will be identified as such and the person will therefore avoid doing them. Maintaining this identity, then, is a psychological element of holding, and the function of the manager of space is to direct all activity in the space towards actions that match the identity derived from the goals, boundaries and degrees of freedom. When activity that does not match the identity of the space takes place with frequency, violates the boundaries, or deviates from the path to the goal, the manager is not fulfilling his or her function in holding the space. The space will lose its identity and correspondingly a measure of its effectiveness.

Every organizational space always maintains, whether intentionally or not, holding processes. Organizational routines, such as individual work meetings, team meetings, management meetings, assessment and feedback processes, etc., are elements of holding. Some of these processes are everyday and routine, such as meeting deadlines, budgets, results and goals. These holding processes are necessary but not sufficient. The most important part of holding is creating the ongoing connection between the organization's goals, boundaries and degrees of freedom, on the one hand, with what is happening in the organization's routine, on the other. I claimed before that the more daring the goals of the space are, the harder it is to accept them and make them a part of the organization's self-conception and identity. In the same breath, I also claimed that this is no reason to simplify the goals. The exact same thing is the case when we speak of boundaries and degrees of freedom. These, too, may at times not be clear enough and arouse opposition, even anxiety. This does not mean one must forfeit them. On the contrary: this is what makes holding

Space for comments & insight

necessary. Goals, boundaries, and degrees of freedom that are not brought up for discussion or aren't questioned periodically are either not challenging enough or simply don't exist in the consciousness of the people in the space. In Chapter 6, I cite two personal stories relating to my work at 'yes'. In the first, I describe how I used the routine setting of meetings in order to connect them with my dreams for the organization. For the entire three years I determined as the timeframe for realizing these dreams, I had to hold them, discuss them, and confront everyone's doubts about them. Not all were realized, but most of the dreams became reality. At the outset, I had to engage in constant holding processes. When we were already on the road to realizing some of the dreams, the dreams stopped being dreams and became goals; consequently, less investment in holding was required.

The most dangerous enemy to holding processes in the space is organizational anxiety about failure. When failure anxiety surfaces, everything becomes urgent. When there is a sense of urgency, pressure, and anxiety about possible failure, it is very easy to give up on values, boundaries, long-term goals and relationships in order to provide a momentary response. Therefore, the key task of the space manager is to maintain the connection to the backbone of the space – the goals, boundaries, and degrees of freedom – without giving in to the temptation of the easy solution during a stressful time or a crisis. Processes of holding in the space are without a doubt an important part of the space manager's accountability, but it is very important to create holding mechanisms independent of him or her. There are many ways of creating holding in space. The first, and most basic, whose importance rises the simpler work in the space is, such as customer service hotlines and sales centers, is the construction of a daily routine. It doesn't really matter how many times it changes. The moment the change occurs, it is necessary to construct a clear, consistent management routine with goals, boundaries, and degrees of freedom. The management

Space for comments & insight

routine must be strict during crises and organizational pressure and may be loosened when the company succeeds and flourishes.

From my personal experience I would like to cite an example in which I was required to engage in holding processes during a crisis in a team I led. In 1987, at the start of my career, I managed a team in the Youth Advancement Department of the Tel Aviv Municipality. The team was responsible for teenage dropouts in three Tel Aviv neighborhoods. The work in these areas was extremely difficult. We dealt with teens, aged thirteen to eighteen, some of whom were already involved in crime. Many were using soft drugs but some were already into hard drugs too. The work was frustrating and the stress level high, mostly because we had to face difficult situations and events. One particular week, during the course of a few days, several terrible events occurred. One boy, a sixteen-year-old, tried to commit suicide while he was in custody, and another, a nineteen-year-old, raped a six-year-old boy and ten-year-old girl in a neighborhood bomb shelter. The team was beset by a sense of collapse and despair. It was clear to me that something had to be done immediately not to lose the team. I called for a staff meeting on Friday (not a regular working day in Israel), and David, one of the youth counselors, offered to host the meeting at his home. At the beginning of the meeting, the participants voiced their despair and wondered about the futility of our work. I was operating completely intuitively; I had little understanding of the topics I cover in this book, but it was obvious that the counselors were sinking and they had to be helped to stay afloat. The purpose of the meeting was to restore the staff members to a point where they would be able to provide counseling and treatment for the teens. Holding the team was not meant to provide a response to its members' needs but rather to the needs of the youths, because a team that is falling apart can't take care of anyone. The first message I made a point of transmitting was that I was not falling apart and that I continued to believe in what we were doing. My own self-doubts,

Space for comments & insight

conclusions about the path we had chosen, thoughts about alternate paths – none of these had a place at this meeting. I allowed the staff members to vent their frustrations but I also insisted that they identify the successes they had had in recent months. This was a simple, transparent exercise that had great results. This type of crisis invited preoccupation with feelings, and I made room for that, because, as I've said, holding without containing doesn't work. But, at the same time that I allowed the counselors to vent frustrations, I didn't allow the staff to dig into them, because the purpose was to hold the goals.

Shifting to less a dramatic environment we can extrapolate from the above to the world of customers' service. Many organizations with customer call centers, which usually employ young people at the start of their professional careers, are in the habit of holding days of fun and social events for their employees. It would be an error to think that these activities serve as type of holding and that they are a way to handle the stress of service reps. Holding takes place when people speak of the difficulties, contain the frustration, and define the goals anew, i.e., restore the meaning of the work. Days of fun and social events are excellent for social cohesion and also as a means of rewarding employees, but their contribution to the holding process and to confronting stress and burnout is negligible.

Containment in Management

The concept of containment is taken from psychology where it is often discussed in the context of child development and psychological treatment. In the setting of the philosophy of space management, I will allow myself to unite the many aspects of this complex concept into a simple paraphrase that may serve us as managers.

Space for comments & insight

Every company and organization contains concerns, fears, beliefs, pressures, anger, jealousies, competition, aggression, and more. Some play a very important role in the mechanism of organizational survival, just as pain and fear are important to human survival. Others have a destructive effect on the organization's function, just as some anxieties and blind faith can destroy a person's function. The life of an organization is full of fantasies and myths about itself and its destiny. The fantasy and myth may be of different kinds: megalomaniac fantasies and eternal life typical of gigantic companies with long histories of success, or the David-and-Goliath myth of small outfits that fought the giants and won. Such fantasies and myths tend to continue to exist even when reality proves that they are no longer grounded in actuality. The concept of containment as expressed in our model deals with managers' ability to identify the emotions of the people operating in the space, especially anxieties and frustrations, to discount the unrealistic fantasies and myths, and to process them into understanding and an appropriate, effective response in reality. The choice of the word "containment" rather than "processing" has to do with the fact that a manager's job includes being a "container" that doesn't leak "organizational poison," to process any poison, and to return it to the organization as a useful, or at least harmless product.

In order to present and clarify the concept, I shall use an example from family life. It's winter in Israel, and thunderstorms are normal. The youngest boy becomes anxious whenever he sees a bolt of lightning followed by a loud thunderclap that rattles the windows in their frames. The thunder causes the boy to imagine or fantasize destruction, and this arouses a great deal of anxiety. The child has little experience and his thought processes have not developed enough to process the event into a concrete reality that can be handled. The parents – mother and father – are both very calm. They are very familiar with thunderstorms. They know the boundaries and effects. Even if they associate

Space for comments & insight

the phenomenon with fantasies or myths concerning the end of the world, they have been through thunderstorms before and are better connected to reality. Even if anxiety surfaces for a second, it is completely controllable. Therefore, when the anxious child starts crying they are able to calm him down. By contrast, when the source of the noise is a bomb exploding just a few miles from home, the parents' containment is much more difficult because the parents have to confront their own anxiety; they can help their child confront his only after they deal with their own. Undoubtedly, this challenge is much more complex and the parents' capacity for coping is significantly lower. Parents are liable to give in to their own anxieties, thereby amplifying the child's.

An organization is an organism that experiences objective anxieties of survival, subjective anxieties stemming from organization leaders' interpretations of real events, and artificial anxieties serving as a trigger for achievements and aroused in the context of organizational processes, such as performance assessments, salary increases, promotions, and bonuses. When an organization is exposed to any kind of anxiety-inducing event, the experience of anxiety always has a measure of real, concrete fear. However, this anxiety is accompanied by an emotional response whose force is disproportional to the event itself. A very important part of the managers' task is to manage personal and organizational anxieties in their space in a way that will maintain the functioning of the organization. When an emotional response of anxiety accompanying a concrete concern is processed and neutralized, the organization's ability to cope is maintained. When the anxiety is not contained, the ability to cope is damaged. When the anxiety is amplified, it floods the organization and the damage is great.

I shall demonstrate with an imaginary story from the life of an organization. In a management meeting of a certain company, one of the members of the

Space for comments & insight

management was interested in promoting the idea of putting out a company newspaper. The VP of HR said he had appointed a team that was working on producing the paper but didn't know the details. The CEO was discomforted by the fact that the manager was not in control of what was happening in his "home court" and reprimanded him accordingly. The reprimanded manager was made to feel anxious and immediately upon the end of the meeting started checking up on every little project happening in his space. Now, it's obvious to all rational people that the production of an internal newspaper is hardly critical in the life of an organization and its coming out late hardly represents a critical existential or functional threat to the company. This is precisely the type of space that the VP of HR can leave in the hands of a more junior officeholder in his unit and cede day-to-day control of. Yet due to the CEO's response, he held working meetings with every manager and project leader, received updates on the state of every project, and even demanded a further update before every management meeting. The VP of HR instructed his secretary to prepare him a weekly report that would summarize all updates of all the projects for him to bring to every management meeting. The burden – for the VP, his secretary, and all the managers in the space – snowballed. Managers and team leaders prepared reports and presentations and everyone felt safer and calmer, despite the fact that a significant portion of the organization's capabilities was being invested in reporting rather than in doing. Our VP of HR could, of course, have reacted differently during that initial management meeting, which would have prevented the amplification of the anxiety and its transmission to the rest of the organization. He could simply have said, "If it seems important to you that we deal with this, I'd be happy to bring you an update at the next meeting or send you an update by email. However, I recommend that we not waste our time on this. We agreed on the concept, timeframe and budget at the start, and I've left my people all the degrees of freedom to operate within these boundaries. I know

Space for comments & insight

we're within these boundaries; otherwise, on the basis of the summary with the person in charge of the project, he would have reported to me." In the first hypothetical scenario, the manager became a conduit, perhaps even an amplifier, of the basic organizational anxiety of losing control. In the second, he contained the anxiety – his own, his CEO's, and the management's – of loss of control. The second scenario prevented the anxiety from being transmitted to the parts of the organization subordinate to the VP, and the energy in the space remained focused on doing.

This example represents an insignificant occurrence in the life of an organization. Its ramifications on the organization's abilities are, of course, limited, but at times events can arouse natural, even justified, anxieties about a failure that is liable to affect the organization greatly. In critical cases, management's ability to contain organizational anxiety means the difference between collapse and effective coping. If we examine the processes that took place in companies during the current economic crisis, we may identify three patterns of response and management of organizational anxiety:

1. Withdrawal, reducing activity, reducing freedom of action in a reflexive manner. In my work in organizational consultancy, I have encountered many companies that reduced their scope of activity in training and organizational development even though their income had not been affected at all, as in the case of large, well-to-do organizations for which these expenditures were negligible, or organizations whose income was not at all affected, such as organizations with government or municipal budgets. Such reflexive action may be an act designed to create an image or may be an expression of anxiety.
2. Continuing regular activity in light of market demands as an adaptive act. Some companies continued to operate on the basis of their ability and

Space for comments & insight

a realistic assessment of the implications of the crisis on their income forecasts, using appropriate caution and consideration. A proper process of containment allows for realistic adaptation to a changing marketplace.
3. Taking advantage of the organization's anxiety to cut back and increase efficiency under the cover of necessity as a manipulative act, i.e., managements that managed to contain their anxiety very well indeed but, instead of containing it at the organizational level and calming the people operating in the space, exploited the anxiety to make cuts they had avoided in the past. In practice the response caused heightened anxiety within the organization.

The sources of anxiety in an organization are many, some being real and concrete, such as the economic crisis, and some psychological and cultural, such as the example above of the internal company newspaper. It has been my experience that in many cases the personal anxiety of managers or employees who are not handling their tasks or have failed to handle them is disproportional to the real organizational damage caused. Every time anxiety becomes dominant, space dies. Containment means controlled management of organizational anxiety. When an organization is capable of containing its anxieties, energy becomes available for realistic concerns and appropriate action, making it possible to preserve the spaces and to keep the organization's effectiveness from being compromised. As the ability to contain organizational anxiety decreases, so rises the preoccupation with reporting, presentations, camouflage and concealment.

It is important to distinguish between containment and denial. Saying, "Everything's fine, there's nothing to worry about, business as usual," does not necessarily constitute containment but may well express denial and disconnection from reality. Denial doesn't save energy. On the contrary:

Space for comments & insight

denial mechanisms require a great deal of personal and organizational energy. Containment always involves identifying the problem, analyzing its true significance, choosing a way to respond, and calming the anxieties. Nevertheless, I don't preach organizational calm, and worries or concerns aren't a bad thing. Organizational pressure, in its positive sense, is usually a necessity. This type of pressure may express itself in excitement and the joy of creation, or in a high degree of commitment and a sense of achievement. When the pressure causes a sense of loss of control, fear of failure, and stress, the pressure is negative for the organization and its personnel.

The Task of Containment in Space

The function of the manager in containment in space is to identify the true emotions within it and manage them within boundaries that are not destructive to the organization or its people. Although we try to live in a rational world not affected by feelings and many of us even believe they succeed in doing so, the world of emotions has crucial influence on our daily decisions and choices within the organization. We have a hard time distinguishing when our response to reality is consistent and appropriate to reality and when it is an over-reaction or under-reaction caused by personal or organizational sensitivity. Anxiety, fear of failure, and fear of social rejection all paralyze human capital at the important levels of talent, creativity, personal values and personality. The more the deep levels of human capital are allowed expression in an organization, the greater the variety and richness of the organization's repertoire and consequently also its effectiveness. A working environment dominated by failure anxiety will paralyze that human capital. Therefore, the manager's job is to contain the fears and anxieties, process them, and turn them into harmless energy. The anxieties and fears closest to managers are their own. Moreover, working in a model

Space for comments & insight

of space management itself, constantly arouses the anxiety of losing control because space management puts the manager on a path of growing concession of control of details and room in the space. Therefore, the first anxiety managers must contain and whose effect they must regulate is their own. Sometimes controlling one's own anxiety is enough to create space.

During the time I was VP of HR at 'yes', there were plans for a workshop for the expanded management forum of the company. According to the plan, during the first part of the workshop every manager would be asked to create a sign s/he'd use to sell his or her wares – his/her activity in the organization. After the signs were supposed to be ready, the plan was for three 20-min. rounds in which the managers were to be paired up randomly, present their wares to one another, and try to find a way in which they could contribute to one another in their routine work. After that, participants were supposed to be asked to sit in small groups and present their work in the organization by means of an art-like plastic display. For this to happen, many arts and crafts materials – fabric, paints, and so on – were made available. None of the people planning the workshop had ever experienced this type of activity. The manager of organizational development managed the entire process and production in a very professional manner, as was her wont, but the entire exercise aroused anxiety within us and the management. The organizational development manager also had an alternate program in case of failure. The management itself was very anxious and kept putting pressure on me to provide more and more details about the planned activity.

The eve of the workshop was very distressing to me. I was stressed and anxious. But it was also clear to me that if I showed up at the workshop like that, any mishap would totally derail me. I went over the program again and tried to identify the spots that were liable to give rise to mishaps, until I felt

Space for comments & insight

we were ready for any scenario. However, life is life, and one can never be prepared for everything. When we gathered in the meeting room of the hotel where the broader management was supposed to participate in the workshop, we discovered that the hotel was hooked up to the TV service offered by our competitor, something our organizational development manager had forgotten to check. This aroused a tremendous amount of anger within the management. The CEO told me that he was going to start the workshop with a sharp reprimand of the HR division. We felt terrible. I was furious with the organizational development manager who, despite clear directives to the contrary, had, of all hotels, chosen this one. I was angry with myself for not checking up on her. To use the language of this book and the philosophy of management I'm presenting in it, I wanted to send the space to hell and attack every last detail of the workshop to make sure there were no foul-ups – something that was too late in any case. But more than anything else I wanted the earth to open up and swallow me. I was so overwhelmed with anxiety that I was almost paralyzed. Nevertheless, I understood that there was no real, imminent threat and that nothing truly bad was taking place. Not really. The event, which aroused the anxiety, was not relevant in any way to achieving the goals of the workshop. However, the response to this irrelevant event could have been extremely damaging to the atmosphere and the people's willingness to engage in an unfamiliar process.

The first thing I did was understand and internalize the last paragraph, i.e., contain my own anxiety about the organization's anger being directed at me and my sense of failure, and not let them overcome me. The next step was to persuade the CEO that reprimanding the HR division at the start of the workshop would cause real damage to the team's ability to run the workshop and the expanded management's willingness to be exposed to an unfamiliar process, causing the workshop to fail. It is clear to me now that had I not

Space for comments & insight

been able to identify my own anxiety and contain it and had I not been able to recognize my failure and understand the extent of its effect, I would not have been able to calm the CEO, the CEO would have reprimanded my team and me, and the workshop would have been a failure. In the end, the CEO did not reprimand the HR personnel for the choice of the hotel, the workshop went according to plan, the managers had a great time, and the workshop achieved the desired results.

The second job of the manager is to contain other people's anxieties. How? First, as noted above, it is necessary to be able to identify anxiety when one sees it, for anxiety has many faces. At the level of the organizational response, it is possible to identify anxiety in a lack of belief in the possibility of succeeding at the task or in a sense of being trapped and paralysis after a failure. At times anxiety is expressed in busy-work, creating an untrue sense of control (anyone who saw the truly unimportant movie *Waterworld* with Kevin Costner may remember the scene in which the leader of "the smokers" – the bad guys in the film – stands on the bridge of the burning ship, which is about to explode, and at this terminal point says to his assistant "Don't just stand there, kill something!"). At 'yes' we always needed new salespeople, but the ads in the newspapers' job section never produced enough candidates. The natural tendency of the recruitment people was to over-react in an unfocused manner – contacting many placement agencies, advertising on a large number of Internet channels, embarking on "friends-bring-friends" campaigns, and taking every other imaginable step. But the over-reacting was primarily expressed in lowering the standards when sorting the applications and increasing the number of people invited for interviews. The bottom line was a great deal of activity with limited results. But a sense of control was generated and the anxiety was less apparent. Clearly, activity is necessary, and deciding whether it constitutes over-reacting or appropriate activity depends

Space for comments & insight

on circumstances. However, one must take care to distinguish between doing something because "something has to be done" and doing something that is in fact required. The job of the space manager is to identify the anxiety, give it its due place, and say, "Let's stop a moment before we start shooting in all directions, look at the practical significance of the failure, and do what we have to do." To avoid organizational over-reaction, the manager using the space management approach needs to contain the organizational anxiety and process it into a realistic concern.

The third job is to construct a culture of containment and containment mechanisms that do not depend on the space manager in person. It is therefore important to create processes and a culture of containment in the space, and not rely solely on the manager's containment ability. Although I generally do not like committees, they are one of the best tools for containment, if only because they keep managers from responding intuitively and immediately. At 'yes' there was a very large fleet of company vehicles and for the most part they were driven by very young drivers, salespeople and technicians. Naturally, there was a lot of damage to the vehicles, and in some cases neglect in maintenance, costing the company very dearly. The vehicle unit tried to handle the phenomenon punitively. Decisions about penalties made without the presence of the offending employee or his/her manager aroused a great deal of anger and resistance, and certainly did not lead to the desired results. I proposed establishing a committee to clarify such events, to be comprised of the employee, an HR rep, the employee's manager and the vehicle officer. In the committee, employees had the opportunity to air their side, and each one of the other participants could make his/her suggestions. The vehicle officer was the committee chair and the decision was ultimately affected by his stance, but the balance in the committee created an appropriate response and the employees given the opportunity to present their position were more

Space for comments & insight

easily able to accept the committee's decision. I don't mean to suggest that the very establishment of the committee solved the problem of bad driving and maintenance of company vehicles, but it undoubtedly contributed to reducing the scope of the problem and certainly prevented the anger that had been present earlier.

It is important to note that the organization adopts the model of the space manager's attitude fairly quickly because of the well-known, familiar processes of leader influence. The influence of a leader who allows a lot of space for others and does not place him/herself in the center in every organizational endeavor is not less, and may be even more than that of a leader who takes up all the space. An example of the effect of holding and containing ability of a leader is evident from the period in which Ofer Bloch managed 'yes'. When I started working for the company, the organization was in the midst of an economic crisis. Before I joined the company, the organization had no holding or containing ability and was incapable of maintaining a uniform direction for even a single year. One business plan came hot on the heels of another, and none was ever followed. Ofer Bloch took over about three months before I was recruited. I won't presume to be the person to evaluate Ofer Bloch's capabilities, but it was obvious to all that in addition to his many great qualities as CEO, he also brought unusual holding and containing abilities to the company. The organization, which until then had been managed erratically in a way that made it impossible to construct proper organizational infrastructures or persevere in a certain direction arousing over-reactions to every event, underwent a revolution in terms of its outlook. With the exception of extreme cases, Ofer did not hurry to respond and left managers space in which to cope. He maintained the boundaries of the company's working program and contained, calmed and examined deeply all doubts along the way. He gave room and great respect

Space for comments & insight

to all his managers and hardly ever imposed anything on anyone. He brought with him a set of organizational values that had been missing in the company and assimilated it immediately. During his tenure, the organization became more founded on technological, organizational and particularly value-laden infrastructures that created a base from which the company took off to where it is in today. I am not judging the management that preceded Ofer. At times, different management styles are needed for different eras. But there is no doubt that Ofer Bloch, almost on the basis of his personality alone, had a tremendous effect on the company's character and culture, making 'yes' an organization with holding and containing abilities far superior than it had ever had before.

Containment and Unmanaged Spaces

Standard, linear growth, taking place along previously known and prepared scaffolding and planned according to yardsticks of meticulous preparation and prior examinations of return on investments, is limited. I am not for a moment denigrating its importance, for it is the basis of any successful company. However, from the start, it narrows the possibility for breakthroughs and creativity. If we examine the development of Israel's flagship company, Teva Ltd., we will see that its great success came from areas of economic uncertainty rather than from the safe spots. Although Teva is based on generic medications, an area in which the risk would seem to be low, it leads the market thanks to risks it assumes, such as challenging medications whose protection under patent law can be challenged, and thanks to the company's flagship medicine, Copaxone. I assume that had Teva decided to go only for the sure thing it would not have reached the economic standing it enjoys today. Breakthrough growth usually happens in the discomforting areas of

Space for comments & insight

uncertainty. Working with balanced budgets, detailed business plans with clear, and agreed-upon models of return on investment, reduce the exposure to risk to the same extent that they reduce the exposure to opportunity.

At Soda Club, a story circulated among the managers, claiming that before Peter Weisberg, the entrepreneur and CEO of the company, entered the German market with the seltzer-making device, he ordered a market study that would examine the chances of the device in this market. The study recommended not entering the German market with this device, because Germans don't drink tap water. For readers unfamiliar with the device, I will say that there is no point in buying a device for making seltzer if you're buying bottled water. It's simply easier to buy the seltzer to begin with. Therefore, the company was distributing the device only in countries where it was common to drink tap water. According to the story, Peter Weisberg said that Germans don't drink tap water only because they don't drink water at all, only seltzer. He went ahead and launched the product in Germany, and the German market became the company's main market, with sales turnover reaching some $120 million. In this context, I would highly recommend reading Nassim Taleb's books, *Fooled by Randomness: The Hidden Role of Change in Life and in the Markets* and *The Black Swan: The Impact of the Highly Improbable*. Taleb's books deals with the extent to which people allow exceptional events to occur in their world, his key claim being that the greater the space allowed for the exceptional to occur, the more likely it is for opportunities and risks to present themselves.

The ability of a leader to head chaotic spaces in tandem with organized ones makes that leader into a producer of perpetual forward motion. Unmanaged or chaotic spaces can be talented people without defined jobs or loafers who wander around the organization asking irritating questions. Chaotic spaces

Space for comments & insight

are also created when the boundaries aren't sufficiently clear, allowing the people for whom lack of boundaries and chaos are a trigger for creativity to express themselves. Managers who can contain uncertainty and allow semi-chaotic areas to exist can create added value for the organizations from these places. For a while, a chemical engineer wandered around Dead Sea Periclase like a bum, busying himself with nonsense. He would bother the secretaries, the payroll accountant, and anyone who had time to listen to him. One day, I asked the plant manager why he didn't just fire him. His answer was that every few months or so this engineer would come to him with an idea worth hundreds of thousands of dollars to the company, and that therefore, as far as the manager was concerned, he was welcome to bother anyone at any time.

Space for comments & insight

The Idea of the Vision in the Space Management Model

In this chapter I would like to discuss the concept of the organizational vision and the feelings and ideas this arouses in me as a manager. In all the positions I held during my career, I "knew" what directed me, where I was going, and what I wanted to achieve. I added quotation marks to the word "knew" because the form or nature of that knowledge is still unclear to me. It was certainly not a methodical process of study and the results of that knowledge were not formulated until the later years of my career. The process was mainly intuitive and I focused on it mostly when assuming a new position. I didn't hurry into action but rather allowed myself a period of immersion, designed in part to gather concrete information about the company's products, their advantages and demerits, the business plan and the structure of expenditures and profits, the organizational structure and the working processes. But most of the learning entailed observing and investigating the social and psychological structure of the company, the manner of operation of its managers, and especially that of the CEO. On the basis of this observation, I would try to understand the world or the perception of reality on the basis of which the company was operating. Using these insights, I would draw a "picture" of my place in the organizational process for the coming years. I would draw a mental picture consisting of words, pictures and composition –

Space for comments & insight

in part intellectual and in part intuitive. That mental picture, or vision, which I would construct, was the result of understanding the organization's needs, goals and challenges. For my own use, I formulated the role the job I was hired to do was supposed to play in the organization and the contribution I could have in this role. As part of the process of learning, I would identify the unique values I could bring. It took a long time until I learned to give verbal, formulated expression to this mental picture. And even when I was able to, the words were just a part of what I saw.

The representation of the future that I made for myself and the spaces I was managing in my different jobs always contained a structural foundation of goals, means and people, in the form of a complex picture of a new world that would be created once the goals were achieved. It also included some foggy transitions and unclear territories because mountains and creeks must be crossed before the fulfillment of the vision. Then all is spread out in front of our eyes. The mental picture, this vision guiding my way, was of the entire space, including its boundaries and freedoms, and its atmosphere and relationships within the boundaries and with the world in which it was operating. I envisioned the future I wanted to get to and this future was limited by time. Today, in light of the current era, it is clear to me that a vision cannot serve its purpose unless it is delimited by time. Given our pace of life and events, time limits are critical, first as creating an area for space and second as a ruler indicating milestones.

When I developed an in-depth familiarity with the concept of vision in the business world, I felt that it lacked two dimensions: the emotional element and pacing, or time. These two are most important in making sure that the vision makes a contribution of real impact on the organization. Without the emotional connection of people to the vision and without the ability

Space for comments & insight

to sense the dimension of time within it, it has hardly any effect at all. And so, when a vision is presented before company employees, it is usually a text without an animating spirit, imagination or energy, a vision without a plastic or metaphoric representation, a mass of words in which often the goals aren't even articulated clearly. The vision in the business world has ignored its artistic and emotional qualities and thereby ceded the energy it is supposed to generate.

In the corporate world, a vision is constructed by means of a technical process in which the management analyzes the organization's goals and formulates a complex technical formula of a vision. After the process of writing concludes, the company's HR section generates nicely designed posters that are hung throughout the company and whose contents are displayed on the plasma screens hanging in the hallways. Usually, the launch of the vision is accompanied by an impressive ceremony, and that concludes the process of constructing the vision and engaging with it. From time to tome, someone will mention the vision at a well-attended conference and it may be brought up in the annual report, but other than that we may say that this more or less concludes the process.

During the first months of working on this book, I searched for vision statements on many company websites in order to demonstrate my thinking about vision. I finally settled on the vision of Teva Ltd. I chose this one because Teva is Israel's flagship company and one of the leading pharmaceutical giants in the world, and I have no doubt that the best managers, consultants and experts are responsible for the formulation of its vision. About a month ago, when I was working on the final version of the book in preparation for its going to print, I went back to Teva's website to see if the vision I had seen there two years ago was unchanged. I discovered that the vision was different

Space for comments & insight

now and that it was in fact embodying some of the ideas I touch on in this chapter. But rather than starting from the end, I shall now present matters by first relating to Teva's vision as it appeared on the website two years ago:

> Teva is a global pharmaceutical company based in Israel. Its vision is to become one of the leading pharmaceutical companies in the world by being the uncontested leader in the generic drugs worldwide and by global development of selected innovative products based on Israeli science.
>
> Teva sets itself apart by combining generic with specific activities, by having strategic depth stemming from vertical integration, by responding to local customer needs while utilizing its global advantage, and by successfully managing the growth in complexity and profitability.
>
> Our success lies in the leadership of its management, the skills and dedication of its employees, the high quality of the products, services and knowledge the company offers, and the focus on the needs of patients and customers.

This vision is clearly formulated, following all the rules. Nonetheless, I would like to examine the extent to which the goals included in the vision are in fact clear. Obviously, Teva set its goal as being "one of the leading pharmaceutical companies in the world by being the uncontested leader in the generic drugs worldwide," surely a fine, respectable goal. But Teva also wanted to insert "global development of selected innovative products based on Israeli science" into the vision. Beyond the fact that no timeframes are determined for this

Space for comments & insight

vision and it is unclear whether Teva will meet its vision even it takes sixty years, I am completely at a loss what the goal is concerning the development of innovative drugs. What role do they play in the mix of products and in the fulfillment of the vision? Anyone familiar with Teva knows that Copaxone plays a very important role in company profits and an even more important role in establishing Teva's reputation. However, the vision statement seems to imply that the development of innovative drugs is secondary to the company being a world leader in the field of generic pharmaceuticals. Can Teva researchers involved in developing innovative drugs lean back because their responsibility for the fulfillment of Teva's vision is lesser compared to the personnel involved in developing the generics? Or perhaps they bear a greater responsibility because the clock is ticking on Copaxone's patent. Does the vision statement make it clear to Teva personnel what is required of them? What goals and vision are they supposed to derive for their units and what would constitute a contribution on their part? Perhaps Teva is already the undisputed world leader in generic drugs? How do you define "leader" anyway? Turnover in dollars? Profitability? Market share? And has this goal been achieved? If so, will a different goal be set? Is there any sort of statement about the type of organization Teva will be once the goal is achieved? And can someone explain to me, in plain language, what the bold part of the following sentence means, "Teva sets itself apart by combining generic with specific activities, **by having strategic depth stemming from vertical integration, by responding to local customer needs while taking full advantage of its global advantage, and by successfully managing the growth in complexity and profitability**"? This vision, like many other vision statements, is formulated too complexly for my taste, and lacks straightforwardness. It certainly doesn't touch either one's imagination or emotions. Furthermore, as it is not delimited by concrete goals and a timetable, it is not actually committed to anything.

Space for comments & insight

The vision is an ancient tool with some primary features. Tribes of hunters would prepare themselves for battle or the hunt with a ceremonial process involving visions. They would dance the story of the coming hunt and reach a point of physical and psychological ecstasy. The story of the hunt would always end with victory and abundance. Early man even painted the story of the hunt on his cave walls. These caves were completely dark, so it is safe to assume the paintings weren't done for the sake of decoration or artistic expression, but were rather a concrete attempt to get a favorable response to the needs of the tribe and the promise of plenty.

For a vision to be alive and active, it has to be a picture of the future, a living, multi-dimensional picture with smell, taste, color and feeling, a kind of futuristic film, a space in which all the players can see the effect of their work and themselves. The vision must include the way in which the vision is going to be achieved, an account of what happens once the vision is achieved, and the effects that achieving the goals will have on the organization, the business environment, and perhaps even society as a whole. The goals in the vision of meta-space – and Teva Ltd. as an example is in fact a meta-space – must allow each of the secondary spaces to create its own appropriate system of goals and vision to serve the vision of the meta-space. All of these must first of all contain concrete goals as well as a representation of the future defined in time with pictures, energy and emotions. Without these, the vision is meaningless. A vision that is too general and whose validity remains constant does not challenge; it is also impossible to assess the extent of its fulfillment. Teva Ltd. is undoubtedly the leading pharmaceutical company in the world in the field of generic drugs but it is currently threatened by proprietary drugs. As I was writing these lines, I thought that Teva should challenge itself with a more up-to-date vision, and to set time limits and limit the vision so that it may be possible to say that it has been realized, and then

Space for comments & insight

forge ahead to the next vision. Our lives in general, and our business lives in particular, move fast. Thus, a vision lacking the dimension of time loses its relevance. As I noted above, after I analyzed and wrote about Teva's vision in the formulation I found two years ago, and trying to stay true to the principle of time and pace, I revisited Teva's website and found that the vision had been changed. When I read the current statement, I was happy to see a reinforcing of my thinking and answers to many of the questions I raised regarding the earlier vision statement. Here is the current version:

> At the beginning of 2010, Teva published its business strategy, reflecting the beliefs and expectations of the board of directors to continue to lead the company through excellence, the willingness to change, appreciation of simplicity, and the approach that, "We are all Teva." This strategy also takes into account global trends, the arena of competition, income, expected profits and our competitive advantages, in order to reach the following goals by 2015:
>
> - Doubling income from $13.9 billion (2010) to $31 billion.
> - Maintaining our M&A strategy.
> - Increasing market penetration and market share in all regions, while focusing on the needs of the local markets.
> - Developing innovative original drugs and specialized niche products.
> - Launching new technologies and advanced processes of development, manufacturing and marketing of generic drugs.
> - Maintaining the segmented manufacturing ratio of 70% generics to 30% branded.
> - Maintaining uncompromising quality standards in every activity!
> - Encouraging financial growth and a global chain of supply.

Space for comments & insight

This vision statement includes the time limit – the year 2015, a clearer goal – $31 billion, and a clarification of the parameter being used as an index – sales volume, and the mix of generic versus proprietary drugs is clear. Furthermore, the metaphoric, emotional and artistic piece appears at the top of the website page: there is a picture of a compass and a few words to which it is very easy to connect on an emotional level: "We make quality healthcare accessible around the world."

Constructing the representation of the future, or vision, of the space is not a one-time deed, but rather an ongoing activity that requires a lot of managerial attention, because the representation is an expression of all the variable parameters in the space – i.e., the goals, boundaries, and degrees of freedom.

When I was a student in the organizational consulting program using the systems psychoanalytical approach, we engaged in an exercise called, "a history of the future." In the context of this exercise, we were asked to construct a scenario of events that moved from the desired future back to the present. The concept of a scenario spoke to me more than the concept of vision. For one, it has time limits. The future is not somewhere out there but rather a defined boundary that exists already in the present. It has many elements of reality that, even if not fully known, are not totally shrouded in mystery. One can assume that there will be opportunities and possibilities and crossroads of decisions; in addition, there are boundaries and alternatives to check. The other group was asked to construct a history of the future in which the group envisions failure, and plot out the process on that basis. I have already mentioned the concept of future oriented management, which means that every decision is based on the steps to come rather than on steps already taken. All the visions I ever operated on were based on working programs that were constructed from the future to the present. Every one of

Space for comments & insight

us uses this approach when packing for a trip abroad: one puts everything one will need at every stage of the journey into the suitcase. Of course errors of prediction happen, such as wrongly forecasting the weather in one's country of destination. But when we speak of organizational forecasting, things are much more complex and the extent of uncertainty goes up the more challenging the vision is.

To give the presentation of the vision impact and organizational meaning, the managers must allow its components to be processed while constantly examining and adjusting them to a changing reality, the organizational and business dynamics, and the changing human elements. From time to time, it must be adapted and tweaked for greater accuracy. The presentation of the vision must never fall into the strangling trap of cold formulations printed in fancy format on high-gloss paper or displayed on electronic boards as a digital text at the company's front entrance. Constructing a full vision incorporating concrete challenges reveals a picture of the space, its boundaries and degrees of freedom to the management, on the basis of the structural architecture of the space.

In my opinion, the central problem with the current understanding of vision is quite simple: an organization cannot have a vision. The ability to produce, think and experience a vision is a human ability. I assume that every human being has some ability to create almost automatically a vision for him- or herself. Leaders have the ability to create a vision for the group; some managers have the ability to create a vision for their space. The managers who led their organizations to extraordinary successes, those who served as the inspiration for those studying the field of management who determined that the basis for these people's success was their vision, were visionaries whose visions filled them with drive, and this drive was contagious and swept

Space for comments & insight

others up. But after 20 years of management among people, some of whom had vision while others did not, I have come to the conclusion that the ability to come up with a vision is not an organizational feature and not within the ability of every manager. Moreover, because the vision has temporary validity and meaning, when the individual who had the vision fades in the history pages of the organization – be it a nation, a company, a school or a senior citizens' home – and when those who shared the vision and the work also fade from view, the vision fades with them. I say this not with the sadness of loss but out of the awareness that that is how it is.

We thus return to the architecture of the space. Every manager, at every management level, can construct his or her space and manage it. Every construction of space serves the technical pieces of the vision and, to my mind, does so better than the vision statement itself, because they require constant updating. However, the full vision, the touching, inspirational one, the one that can pull people along in its wake, will always belong to one person or a small group of people who share the passion and can inspire others to follow. The next chapter will deal with the functional manager and the differences between that and the mythological manager. I would however already like to say that the mythological manager, the one with the vision, will work towards fulfilling that vision and not leave any room or allow the insertion of other visions, whereas the functional manager will incorporate other visions into his/her own as much as possible as long as the central vision does not lose its essence.

Space for comments & insight

The Space Manager or The Functional Manager

The model of organizational space management presents a desirable situation in which there are as many degrees of freedom and as few boundaries as possible. The model invites managers to grant their personnel a lot of freedom and not waste their time on control and monitoring, but rather focus on creating value for the organization. In this process, managers must cede some of the room they take up in the space and their centrality in it and give room and importance to their people, not as playing at *noblesse oblige* but as seeing others' importance as being at least equal to their own. Such managers see themselves as having functions or a job, not as the be-all and end-all. They are not a different type of manager, but they do have a different way of seeing the job of management. Every manger can adapt to whatever degree suits him or her the management approach present in this book, if only because this approach does not insist on all or nothing. This model does not call for a revolution but rather for a developmental process. The most important thing is to understand that the requirements of the manager are changing and that s/he is confronting a different set of expectations.

That being said, it is important to note that there are management patterns, ways of looking at the world, characteristics and personal tendencies that can help bring individuals closer to this approach. It is fairly obvious that, on the basis of an understanding of space and this model of its management, the mythological manager who is present, charismatic, dominant, and who knows all and solves all problems, may contradict the very process of the development of the organizational space and the people operating within it. This is not to say that a space manager is not required to be charismatic, have presence and great influence, and be a figure worthy of respect. On the contrary: in order to create a representation of the vision of the space and generate belief in that vision, in order to set the goals and the boundaries and grant them validity, to enable a manager to contain the organization's

Space for comments & insight

anxieties, the manager must be forceful and charismatic and possess highly developed interpersonal skills. The essential difference is manifested in the extent of the manager's presence. The presence of a space manager in the space with all of his/her abilities, personal forcefulness and charismatic personality must be properly titrated. His/her presence must not decrease the presence of others in the space. The ability of the manager to be present enough when s/he needs to be and absent enough when this is possible is a very important parameter and can be learned.

From my own experience, I will say that managing one's own presence in the space is not an easy task. Western culture in general, and management culture in particular, as well as the natural desire of every human being, steer us towards being in the center of every matter or event. An organizational development manager at 'yes' once told me that I am "confusing," at times difficult and demanding but at other times giving a great deal of freedom and almost absent from the process. Indeed, it was not easy for me to cede my presence, for two reasons: one, I wanted the way to be my way, and the other, the human need to be present. I learned very quickly the price of over-presence and I taught myself to clear the stage if I wanted things to happen even in my absence. After all, if everything has to happen on the basis of your taste and choice and presence, you will have to be present every place every time and nothing will happen without you. Moreover, if you are always present you will block your people's abilities and prevent the expression of their human capital. It is important to note that except in some extreme cases of personality construction and management style everyone can learn gradually to concede control and monitoring. Nevertheless, it is clear that there is a predisposition to one direction or the other, and the more that this direction points to space management the easier it will be to internalize the approach.

Space for comments & insight

Functional Management

I mentioned the theories of needs conceived by Maslow and his followers in the first chapter. According to these theories, one may divide human needs into two types – needs of dependence versus needs of independence. The needs for physical security, social security, and social esteem, are needs of dependence, while the needs for personal development, self-actualization, achievement and personal empowerment are needs of independence. Every manager or leader is obligated to provide a response both to the needs of dependence and needs of independence of the people operating in the space, but different managers have differing abilities and tendencies in providing a response to the different types of needs.

One can divide managers into two groups on the basis of their tendencies. Those who tend to provide a response to the needs of dependence and even encourage them I shall call mythological managers, while those who tend to provide a response to the needs of independence and even encourage them I shall call functional managers. Some might say that mythological managers may be characterized by having a more narcissistic personality than functional managers, but I am not a psychologist and I shall leave this in the realm of speculation and prefer to focus on patterns that are more visible to the everyday eye.

The functional manager costs little for his/her contribution. S/he does not require adulation and does not need room at the expense of others. S/he encourages people to climb higher and higher mountains and conveys to them and their space a great deal of confidence in the abilities of the personnel as well as high expectation. S/he provides the group and individuals with what they need in order to express their own maximal value for the good of

Space for comments & insight

the group's goals and vision while they derive a sense of satisfaction, value and meaning. S/he echoes the organization's successes and does not hurry to appropriate them to him/herself.

By contrast, the mythological manager is always at the center even when s/he isn't required to do anything. His/her personality is always on display; s/he is always involved in every problem and every solution. The general sense is that without this person nothing ever happens; this sense often reflects reality, though not because the other people in the space are incapable of generating the solutions but because s/he doesn't give other people a chance to conceive of solutions without him/her. S/he is at the center of every process that takes place in his/her organizational space.

One of the organizations in which I worked once held a managers' conference over the course of several days. On one of the evenings the managers went out for drinks at a local bar. The atmosphere in the group was excellent, like among most groups enjoying an evening out. People were eating, drinking, talking and laughing. After about an hour, one of the most senior managers, full of goodwill showed up and took charge. He ordered a round of drinks for everyone and "suggested" everyone play some party games. Within a few minutes, you could see how all present shrank in on themselves to make room for him. I am sure that the manager had no idea what his effect was on the situation. Even in the context of a social event, this manager was incapable of giving the people the necessary space: he just had to fill it all himself.

As a manager's style leans more toward the mythological so rises the cost that the space and people pay. Mythological managers reduce the truth to their truth and put great effort and energy into controlling and monitoring,

Space for comments & insight

i.e., constantly stopping the organization in order to release it. They attribute all organizational successes to themselves, giving little credit to others. The character of an organization is determined on the basis of the manager tending either to the mythological or the functional. At one end of the scale we find an organization without any space at all, managed by the mythological manager under the motto of, "Do what you're told and don't ask any questions," while on the other end of the spectrum we find an organization with many spaces managed on the principle of, "I shall share all my plans, business, economic and legal information with you, and you'll figure out what you can do to help me reach the goals in the best way possible in the context of your job using your knowledge and talent." At one end we have one manager and many employees, some senior and some junior, who have been hired to create an already determined output, in a place that has no interest in their ability to bring any added value to the organization. At the other end we find many partners, some senior and some junior, people who have space for their own inclinations, talents, values, creativity and added value. They can and want to contribute these; they want to make a difference.

In the organization managed by the mythological type of manager, the chance that something will happen that lies outside the scope of the ability or knowledge of the manager is very low. In the organization managed by the functional type of manager, however, the manager's expertise and specific abilities join the total of all the abilities and knowledge of the people in the organization, and therefore the organization's performance will exceed the limits of its managers. The inclination to be functional brings a manager closer to the model of space management presented in this book.

The next parameter characterizing the functional manager is an active internal space and the ability to accept the internal space of his/her people.

Space for comments & insight

The Internal Space of the Functional Manager

I once watched a movie showing how South America natives catch monkeys. They whittle out a deep hollow of a tree trunk, the opening of which is barely large enough for a monkey's paw. They then place a few nuts inside the hollow. The monkey sticks its paw into the hollow and closes its fist over the nuts. Because its paw is now fisted, the monkey cannot withdraw it from the hole. The key to the monkey's freedom lies in its ability to make a very fast change in how it defines its goal: food or freedom? The monkey's inability to understand the conflict between the two goals and create a new paradigm of behavior could cost it dearly; the monkey, in fact, doesn't let of the nuts and pays with its life. We smile at the silly monkey, unable to see how much we, too, are stuck in the same situation, our hands fisted the same way, just because we refuse to let go of our 'nuts'.

The internal space is a function of intellectual, analytical and emotional abilities and a wide range of perspectives. Our culture is one that privileges intellectual, analytical skills and seeks proof, calculations, and well-formulated, grounded forecasts. Our culture privileges the logical, linear and immediate connection between what we do and the results we desire. Real life, on the other hand, is not linear and we don't always understand the logic connecting action and outcome. Our culture encourages us to ignore what we do not understand or cannot quantify, thereby reducing our capacity for observation. Depth and breadth of the perception of reality and alternate perspectives are among managers' most important management tools. Points of view and perspective are not generated by MBA and Economics programs but rather the result of personally expanding one's world of art, philosophy and science, as well as gardening, engineering and literature. A number of years ago, I participated in a drawing class taught by painter Avinoam Kosovsky. The course focused on

Space for comments & insight

the proper viewing of the object being sketched. As a painter, I was used to my brain projecting what it already "knew" onto reality, thereby imposing on my ability actually to see what was in front of me. I was really surprised to see how true this was of me – the extent to which my "understanding" of reality made it harder to see it for what it is. From the moment this tendency was removed and my vision cleared of projections, the sketching itself became a breeze.

Having many perspectives allows us to see several patterns of alternate "realities" simultaneously, all informed by the same collection of data; it even allows us to see data we have not been trained to see. An internal space allows us to see that we operate within existing paradigms and to examine them. An internal space allows us to learn that the way in which we see things is only one of many possible ways to understand reality and that there are alternatives. I think that the movie *What the Bleep Do We (K)now?* should be mandatory viewing in every management program. When we are unaware of the fact that we are operating on the basis of old paradigms or are unaware of the existence of alternatives, we will try to find our way in the maze in which we are lost over and over again using the same insufficient – and, more importantly, incorrect – solutions. We'll recreate the pattern our forebears used on the erroneous assumption that it must be right for us too.

In the first company where I managed the HR department, one of the young, talented production employees was appointed to the position of shift supervisor. Shlomo was industrious, full of good intentions and someone who always strove for excellence. His team consisted of ten workers, one of whom was known as being lazy and generally problematic. The company had a collective agreement and a powerful labor union protecting employees, and the problematic individual could not be fired. Shift supervisors were simply forced to deal with him. Using the available management tools, namely

Space for comments & insight

disciplinary hearings and delayed salary increases. In a conversation I had with Shlomo a few weeks after he assumed his new position, he told me how he intended to handle the lazy worker. He intended to "supervise him to the point where he had no air to breathe," "to stick it to him," to punish him "until he broke." It was obvious to me that Shlomo would not be able to create a change in the conduct of this employee using the standard approach he was planning to use. The solution that was just more of the same or less of the same wouldn't generate change. The problematic worker was used to handling the approach and skilled at it. So I suggested to Shlomo that he reexamine the situation. The man in question was 40 years old. He had been scolded and seen as a disappointment his entire life. He also knew that, were it possible, he would have been let go. His self-esteem was low and the only satisfaction he derived from his work was to drive his managers out of their minds. I pointed out the worker's needs to Shlomo and I suggested he "catch" the guy doing something good and saying something nice to him, though in a low-key, non-gushing way. Shlomo's retort to me was that the guy never does anything good. I asked him if there were days when he didn't cause any damage. He smiled and said yes. "Isn't that good?" I asked. Shlomo, smiled again in agreement. I proposed that, at the end of such a day, Shlomo approach the worker, put a hand on his shoulder, and say, "Well done! We got through the shift without any hassles." Of course, Shlomo was worried and offered many reasons why this plan wasn't going to work and only send a message to the employee that he doesn't have to make any effort. So I said, "We've been trying your way for 15 years and it hasn't succeeded yet. What makes you think it'll work now? Try my way for three months and if it, too, fails, at least we can say we tried something new."

Shlomo decided to work with me. He'd come to me every week and together we'd try to think of ways to give the guy some type of positive feedback.

Space for comments & insight

Once it was by saying that the shift had gone smoothly, another time it was by pointing out that his station was always clean and yet another time was by noting that he was never late. After a while, the problematic worker had completely changed his attitude, and in the next round of salary discussions, to everyone's enormous surprise, he was already up for an increase. The company gained an employee only because a shift supervisor agreed to take a new look at the paradigmatic 15-year old relationship between this problematic employee and management and make the change that was needed.

Without an internal space, we will tend to choose first-degree solutions such as "more of the same" or "less of the same." We will prefer not to make second-degree structural changes and won't even be aware of a third-degree alternative, i.e., rereading reality and adopting a fundamentally different approach. The authors of *Change: Principles of Problem Formation and Problem Resolution* (Paul Watzlawick, John H. Weakland and Richard Fisch) use the example of the American attempt to wage war on the production, transport and smuggling of alcohol during Prohibition. As successes declined, budgets, manpower and political struggles increased. The more illegal alcohol was fought, the more alcohol-related organized crime – smuggling, producing, and selling, increased. The number of victims of alcohol produced without supervision rose from year to year. The solution, of course, was re-legalization. Similarly, today, we worry about the legalization of soft drugs or drugs in general. Countless professionals testify that legalizing marijuana will not only not do any damage but will also cut the amount of hard drugs on the streets and reduce the commercial field for organized crime. In order to reach such a conclusion one must be able to redefine the lines of "good" and "bad."

A company can be locked in a tough price struggle with a competitor and try to differentiate itself on the basis of price to the point where both the

Space for comments & insight

company and its rival lose vast sums and perhaps even their economic right to exists in a fight for the customer's loyalty. By contrast, the same company can choose a reverse strategy of differentiation – "We are expensive because we are better" – or choose a third-degree change and say, "We are both expensive and exclusive; we have no salespeople and are interested in selling only to the select few." Thus, a company can turn its customers into an exclusive club, adding the value of exclusivity to a product bearing an exclusive price tag. I would warmly recommend the book by Prof. W. Chan Kim and Renée Mauborgne, *Blue Ocean Strategy*, which offers a way out of the "red ocean" of fighting over market share and price toward the "blue ocean" of restructuring demand and appropriate supply at the right price, i.e., the supply of value.

The freedom to examine reality as if it is unknown, the freedom to tell yourself, "Don't hurry to 'know' what is going on; give yourself time to observe. Maybe you'll see better if you don't rush to decide, and, instead of deciding, go to lunch and listen to the unease you're feeling as a result of the decision you're about to make, and understand that something in you is trying to tell you that the decision you're about to make is no good," the freedom to reach a wildly unpopular decision and to live with the looks of bewilderment about your idiocy and lack of understanding – all of these construct your internal space or conceptual room for maneuvering that gives you flexibility. The internal space calls on us to provide time, sometimes to let go of control, to allow ourselves to experience uncertainty and stay within processes in a conscious way to deepen our understanding before acting. The internal space requires that we allow ourselves not to be sure. It asks us to accept the reality we see as one possible interpretation from among a number of alternate interpretations, and invites us to understand what they are and examine whether they allow us a greater scope for coping. Some things in

Space for comments & insight

the internal space are allowed that aren't allowed in action. We're allowed to dream an alternate reality without being considered delusional.

Donald Woods Winnicott, the renowned psychoanalyst who specialized in the emotional development of children, notes the tremendous importance of the intermediate space between the imagination and reality in the child's development. The child's ability to imagine, and on the basis of the imagination to examine the possibilities of implementation in reality, allows the child to develop a greater repertoire of behaviors and coping with reality. The internal space is one of imagination, questions and doubts, uncertainty and especially a continuation of personal development and growth. The internal space is capable of containing "organizational fantasies" without rejecting them out of hand.

Someone who views his or her own perception of reality as the be-all and end-all of truth, the only relevant truth around, someone who doesn't recognize self-doubt, will have a very limited internal space and will find it hard to allow others real space; s/he will have a natural inclination toward mythological management.

In order to allow space, one has to believe in the ability of the space to produce positive results rather than disaster. Without such a belief, we will find it hard to allow space. Jacob Burak's book, *Do Chimpanzees Dream of Retirement*, deals with the human evolutionary inclination to prefer the identification of risk rather than the identification of opportunity. This is a relic of a primitive evolutionary need for survival in the wild. Human beings have long since stopped needing this tendency, for it has stopped producing adaptive value in most settings in life and most cultures. Burak also demonstrates how an index of trust positively affects the economic situation of society and economic growth.

Space for comments & insight

The Functional Manager and the tendency for Trust or Suspiciousness

According to Erik. H. Erikson's developmental model, all people undergo a developmental stage in which they adopt a tendency either to trust or to suspiciousness. I have chosen to translate this tendency into a formulation that suits the practical side of life in an organization. According to this formulation, at one end there will be people who tend to trust people and believe that the world creates an infinite number of opportunities, while at the other end there will be people who believe that no one is to be trusted and that the world is a threatening place.

This stance isn't absolute. Even people who tend toward suspiciousness and think that generally people are not worthy of trust and that the world is filled with threats accept as a fact that there are trustworthy individuals and that life also offers opportunities. On the other hand, those who tend to trust people and think of the world a being full of opportunities also accept as a fact that some individuals should not be trusted and that though life offers opportunities it is also necessary to be on guard against risks. The difference lies in the general tenor of the inclination.

If someone tends to believe that "the imagination of man's heart is evil from his youth" (to quote Genesis 8:27) and that the world is filled with dangers, this belief will serve as that person's basic default inclination. But if someone tends to believe that "the imagination of man's heart is good from his youth" and that the world is filled with opportunities, this belief will serve as that person's basic default inclination. On the basis of my own experience – which obviously does not constitute scientific research – people do not change their basic stance. A suspicious person may be moderate, almost perfectly

Space for comments & insight

balanced; his or her attitude could be very close to that of a trusting person. Nonetheless, there will be a clear tipping towards one of the basic poles. At each of the poles it is possible to raise the weight of the contrary stance, but not to change the default setting. Managers who believe in people's basically good nature and that the world is full of opportunities will manage their space of activity in an open, flowing, enabling and supportive way. Such managers will afford larger spaces by reducing boundaries and give more degrees of freedom and independence to their people. Their working meetings with the teams will not be for the sake of follow-up and reporting but rather meetings in which all the participants consider solutions together and create challenges together. Such managers allow their personnel to try things and make mistakes. Their people will seek out new tasks on their own, and when such managers want something in particular they will usually request it rather than issue orders from above. Such managers will feel less threatened by talent in their space.

Managers who believe that the world is a generous place offering more opportunities than risks and that people are basically good will be open to challenges and innovative, groundbreaking action. Such managers will rely less on the experience of the past and be more invested in the future and the horizon it creates. Their tasks will differ from those of their teams; they will be preoccupied not with managing personnel and activities but rather with managing the future and supporting the teams as needed. The conduct of such managers makes the space more enabling and encourages initiatives and breakthroughs, thus being more functional for the organization and its personnel. By contrast, managers who feel that people are fundamentally untrustworthy will manage their space with processes of oversight, control and reporting. Working meetings will be devoted primarily to follow-up on the performance of tasks. They will issue instructions about what to do and

Space for comments & insight

how to do it. The solutions will be their solutions; there will not be much room for disagreement. Their response to opinions that differ from their own will be unpleasant, as if they constituted threats. I am sketching an archetype or schema rather than a real person. In reality, things are more nuanced and complex. But every manager reading these lines knows his or her own heart and inclination. Some manager behavior is learned and can express a belief that is not necessarily anchored in the manager's own personality, making it easier to adopt an alternate mode, but even the most suspicious manager can learn to trust and expand the part of his/her personality that recognizes that despite the suspiciousness it is also possible to trust.

From this discussion of trust and its importance in space management in our model, let us move on to the question of personal freedom and the need for social approval, or freedom from conformity.

The Functional Manager and Internal Permission

In my various positions of HR management I have look at many management candidates at all echelons: CEOs for subsidiaries, Vice Presidents, mid-level management, even junior management. One of the most important qualities I looked for with the help of the various diagnostic agencies with whom I worked and in face-to-face interviews was always the "internal permission" of the candidate. What do I mean by that?

All human beings undergo a central process of socialization as they develop as children in a family and society. The process recurs every time people enter a new society. This process consists of positive and negative feedback

---

Space for comments & insight

that individuals receive from the society in which they live designed to steer individuals towards the beliefs and behaviors considered desirable by that society. We all have a fundamental need for acceptance and we all experience, to one degree or another, a fear of abandonment and loneliness. We therefore direct ourselves automatically towards accepted beliefs and behaviors and steer clear of those that might entail social sanction. The mechanism of socialization is particularly effective when we are young and reaches its peak during adolescence. It tapers off the older we get and the more we learn to approve our own beliefs and behaviors. In extreme cases of this phenomenon we will see people who need approval for every little thing they do – the clothes they wear, the hairstyle they choose, the car they buy, and of course needing approval and instructions for every last thing they do at work. At the other extreme, we find people who ask no one's advice, who consult nobody and don't even keep anyone informed; they just do what they do. The variable parameter among these different types is the measure of internal permission and autonomy versus the measure of conformity and need for external permission.

In most of our jobs in life we need external permission in addition to our internal one. We often need approval from our direct supervisor, and the need for approval isn't in and of itself a bad thing. As in many other instances, the question is only one of extent. In addition, I think it is important to distinguish between the need for external approval or permission and the need for feedback. People who need external permission for their stances and actions will not act or persevere in their positions unless they get approval, or external permission. By contrast, managers who don't need approval, or external permission, but understand that they have what to learn from their environment, can ask for feedback, listen to alternate opinions and examine other ways as part of examining reality before reaching decisions and taking

Space for comments & insight

action. People who receive negative feedback should reexamine their positions and plans, which is not to say that they must change their decisions. The fundamental difference between those who need approval and those who need feedback lies in the nature of the need. The need for external permission stems from dependence on emotional and social security; thus, managers needing external permission will not act unless they feel that their actions are accepted. Such managers depend on their actions being popular. By contrast, the need for feedback stems from the need to test external reality, to test oneself, to internalize alternate stances and plans. The result of receiving feedback, even if the feedback is not favorable, may be sticking to one's guns and continuing with the unpopular plan. Managers who make use of feedback do not depend on it; managers who need external permission depend on it.

Space for comments & insight

Organizational Stories / Case Studies

This chapter presents the manifestations of space management in the life of an organization according to our model and how it can be used as a tool. I have chosen to make this presentation using two organizational processes I led in my last job as Vice President for HR of 'yes'. To do so properly, I shall begin with a short history of the company.

'yes' is a multi-channel satellite television company. It was established in 1998 and aimed to become the leader in terms of product quality and innovation in the multi-channel TV market. The multi-channel TV broadcasters in operation until then had offered a very small selection of programming and bad service. When 'yes' entered the market it did so with a technological advantage, digital service, and a contents advantage, more daring and cutting-edge programming than the offerings of its competitor.

The launch of the new product was accompanied by media fanfare and the first market share was taken by storm. Consumers were prepared to pay more than the rate offered by the competition. The competitor was not left without a response and rapidly started to improve their product. This is when the real battle began, with both companies offering lower rates. The rapid

Space for comments & insight

growth of 'yes' made it impossible to adapt the company's infrastructures to its market, and soon enough confusion and mishaps emerged in the chain of supply, from the moment of the sale to routine service. Customers were forced to wait three months for service installation in their homes, and then too appointments would be rescheduled and delayed and billing would be full of errors. 'yes', a young company that taken off with a tremendously high trajectory with an ambitious business plan, suddenly experienced a sharp drop. Its expenses were estimated on the basis of an optimistic – and unrealistic – forecast of earnings. In short order, the company was forced to cut expenses sharply and painfully.

In order to cope with the difficulties and improve service, the company changed the way it handled customers. From an all-nation professional division (sales, service, and technical support), according to which all customers were getting service in professional areas from a national control center, the company transitioned to a geographical division (north, center, and south), according to which customers got service from the service center nearest to their home. In practice, this meant the establishment of three companies, each headed by a CEO, and each of which provided all the services, from sales through installation to routine service; billing, too, was done on the basis of geography.

Each of the three companies included a sales department, a customer service department, and a technical department. Each one of them had its own accounting and billing department, a local housekeeping manager, and a local HR manager. This change greatly improved working processes and customer satisfaction, and helped to stabilize the company, but from the outset it was clear that the division into geographical areas was a temporary one. Thus, the company started to work towards restoring the original national structure and

Space for comments & insight

the previous divisions, i.e., professional divisions reflecting the company's areas of activity: service, sales, and a technical division. A manager at the level of Vice President was appointed to each one of these divisions, instead of the former CEOs. In addition to this structural change, the HR managers who had been appointed regionally were now appointed to HR managers of the professional divisions: one HR manager for customer service, one for sales, and one for technical support.

The processes and changes described above were very hard on the organization. Fiscal difficulties were translated into a reduction of benefits given to the employees at the outset, including salary cuts and terminations. The many organizational changes, the high rate of turnover of managers, and the ongoing slashing of budgets, created an atmosphere of uncertainty and distrust, which was translated into cynicism, antagonism, and even insubordination. Employee rights were not always properly protected and the general sense was one of constant insecurity and genuine anxiety about the company's future.

When I came on board, in February 2004, the HR division did not exist as a division. Beyond the many transformation that had taken place in HR during the years the company was establishing itself, the division had been left without a manager for about six months. The three operational divisions – customer service, sales and technical support – each had its own HR manager. They reported directly to the professional Vice Presidents and were responsible both for their own professional division and for the geographical location they happened to be in: one was responsible for the north, another for the center, and the third for the south. Company headquarters also had an HR manager and a number of employees who dealt with training and welfare for headquarters personnel – some 500 people.

Space for comments & insight

When I took the job, everything was on the verge of crisis and thus urgent. The company had failed to recruit enough employees for its field sales force. The company lacked many officeholders and management was mainly busy with building a 3-year business plan under the direction of the new CEO, Ofer Bloch, who had taken the job at the end of 2003.

I tried to provide at least a partial response to the immediate demands so that whatever was necessary on a day-to-day basis would actually happen. However most of my time was devoted to learning about the company and the HR division. I identified several main challenges that needed handling in operations, recruitment, employee training, and working norms.

HR operation

The operational aspect of HR was the part that had been called "personnel management" in the past, and it included hiring, informing the salary system, handling employee contracts, managing personal files, and filing documents. All of these are the initial infrastructure of HR, but do not include the more professional aspects, such as training, organizational development, manager support, handling welfare issues, and the like.

The responsibilities of the HR managers included all HR activities. These managers dealt directly with every matter, from publishing wanted ads and operating manpower agencies, through the reporting of new hires to the salary system, dealing with disciplinary issues, supporting management, producing welfare events, updating the salary and bonus systems, and all the way to organizational development, and they did it all with insufficient

Space for comments & insight

personnel. This variety of tasks spread over an impossible range and improper resource planning made full, professional work out of the question. The less attractive but basic operational parts of HR, requiring high degrees of order and organization, were the first to suffer. New company hires were not always inputted into the payroll system and therefore missed their first month's salary, while employees who left the company were not always removed from the payroll system and so received pay for days they hadn't in fact worked. Overtime, absences and sick days were not reported properly or on time, and there were many errors in salaries. HR's conduct with external suppliers was also not problems free. In addition, the company's cash flow was not good, so providers were often paid late. HR suppliers had to wait a long time because administrative processes such as placing orders and approving invoices were done lackadaisically. The situation reached a peak of absurdity when a certain provider agreed to work with the company's customer service division, which paid its debt, but refused to work with the company's sales division.

Recruitment

The company had to struggle with the high rate of employee turnover typical of the industry. These employees, usually at the start of their careers, are looking for a job that will last a year or two after their army service. It was clear that, although it was important to try to get them to stay longer in order to save on recruitment and training, this situation would not change because that was the nature of these jobs.

Although recruitment was a key factor for the success of the company, there was no central body handling it. Rather, each of the three HR managers

Space for comments & insight

managed recruitment for her own division and reported to the manager of the division being served. In the absence of a professional force and an infrastructure for sorting and eliminating candidates, and because the number of responses to the wanted ads was far from enough to meet the company's recruitment needs, recruitment processes relied heavily on the various manpower agencies to send candidates through the selection process. The selection process was primarily based on the assessment centers of an independent diagnostic institute. The selection process was long, exhausting and wasteful; out of a hundred candidates, only one or two new hires survived the process.

The situation created a number of major problems. First, although the assessment was that the company was receiving applications from tens of thousands of candidates a year, there was no system in place that allowed the company to document and follow up on these applications. This caused a lot of confusion and created a situation in which a candidate could submit an application several times, and even get to assessment centers in various parts of the company and in different units, without anyone being able to track the number of times the individual had gone through the process. In addition, it would happen that a candidate was rejected for a job in one location but accepted for the same job in a different place. Secondly, control of the recruitment process did not lie with the company so that it was completely dependent on the manpower companies. In addition, recruitment costs were extremely high because of the payments to the manpower companies for placing employees and because of the many selection stages required, as the percentage of hires was very low.

Space for comments & insight

Training

The next activity representing a challenge for the company was employee training. The sales force and the technicians came to 'yes' without the training to be able to do their jobs and had to learn the company's product, technology, information system and working norms. The training process lasted three to four weeks, and was expensive, both in terms of the trainees' and trainers' salaries and in terms of the effect on the level of company employees' functioning. 'yes' did not have a central body in charge of training; each of the divisions – sales, customer service and technical support – participated in training the new hires. Initiatives for improving training were local and no processes of accumulating training knowledge and expertise were in place for future reference. There was no documentation of courses taking place; the level of the training's effectiveness was not tested; certainly no uniformity of training technique or culture was created. Training budgets were in the hands of the section's managers and investments in management development and organizational culture were also left entirely up to them.

Values, norms and boundaries

Frequent structural changes, high employee and manager turnover, turmoil in the company's financial situation, and anxiety over its very existence led to an abandonment of normative and value driven boundaries. There were cases of vandalism in company offices, irresponsible driving in company vehicles, and many disciplinary violations. Commitment to immediate results caused managers to turn a blind eye to disciplinary infractions so that boundaries

Space for comments & insight

were not put in place where they were needed. At the same time, managers were not sufficiently aware of what was required of them by labor law so that the law was also broken on occasion. As a result, there were many employee lawsuits against the company pending.

Organizational culture and strategy

The company did not have a central professional body in the form of an organizational development manager, and there were no designated resources in the HR structure that could routinely deal with the construction of an all-company organizational culture. There were no organizational processes within HR dealing with a shared management culture and values. There was no way to identify any potential human capital and key people whom it would be proper to develop and retain in the organization.

While identifying challenges in the HR field, I was also examining the company's HR needs in regard to the new 3-year business plan. The recently constructed plan defined a number of major goals:

- Increasing the number of customers through customer recruitment.
- Maintaining existing customers.
- Increasing revenue and profitability per customer.

These goals were and remain the right goals for any Israeli communications company. Therefore, it may be assumed with a high degree of certainty that:

- Competition for workers in customer service and sales would increase and the recruitment costs would therefore rise accordingly.

Space for comments & insight

- A company whose sales and service people were more skilled would have a competitive advantage.
- The company that would be considered the better employer would retain its veteran employees who would constitute its human capital and attract more new candidates.
- In so competitive a market, the company would have to combine a strong backbone with maximal flexibility.

On the basis of this analysis, I defined the goals of the HR division for the next three years:

- The foundation for every HR contribution to the organization would have to represent an immediate improvement to the processes of HR operations, employee intake and dismissal, and accurate attendance and salary reporting. Operations would include the proper and fair construction of relations with HR service providers, including manpower companies, selection institutes, and suppliers in the field of welfare.
- The company would have to be based on its own recruitment and selection mechanism and reduce its dependence on external providers, both in order to control recruitment costs in a reasonable way and in order not to be stuck in situation in which the company was completely dependent on external elements that might not be able to meet company needs.
- It would be necessary to build a training structure that would ensure ongoing improvements in the human capital operating in the company.
- It would be necessary to build a value-based organizational culture that would include clear, firm boundaries that would serve as a stable framework for the company.
- It would be necessary to build an infrastructure for managing recruitment

Space for comments & insight

processes and a national recruitment center that would free the company from its dependence on placement agencies and selection consultants.

After identifying the problems and challenges and after articulating the goals, it was time to define the space and build it according to the data available to me. When I built the HR structure, I allocated resources according to three levels: focused operations at the daily level, more complex operations and leading processes of improving the skills of mid-level management, and management at the highest level, which included managing boundaries, developing a local organizational culture at the mid-level, and leadership of values and strategy.

In the chapter entitled "The Structural Architecture" I presented the principle of the floatation device. According to that principle, when the operational part, which is primarily within the scope of accountability, does not receive the proper response, the entire organization above it sinks in order to deal with these problems. So that it is possible to free up resources to the circle of responsibility, the realm of accountability must be completely fulfilled. I formulated this principle to myself for the first time when I started to build the organizational spaces of HR at 'yes'. In order to promote the area of HR operations and free up the HR manageress from unnecessary tasks, I appointed a HR coordinator in each geographical district, whose activities would focus on: recruitment and new employee intake (working with the manpower agencies and the assessment and selection institute), inputting new hires in the system, handling local welfare activities, and providing logistical and operational assistance to HR projects. These activities did not require highly developed expertise and it would be possible to build an accountable team with a small budget. This force provided concrete, immediate solutions in the field and allowed the HR managers to focus on problem solving, support for mid- and senior-level management, and promoting training and organizational processes.

Space for comments & insight

This change immediately increased the involvement of the HR managers in central processes in the divisions where they worked. At this stage, I had to decide whether to build the unit as a centralized one in which all HR employees report directly to me, or to leave the HR managers in a matrix reporting structure in which they reported to the division managers at the operational level and to me at the professional level. It was clear to me that were I to opt for the decentralized structure, it would be harder for me to exert my authority and assimilate the HR policy derived from my worldview. On the other hand, a centralized structure would decrease the general impact of HR. I opted for the matrix structure in order to guarantee to status of the HR managers in the divisions they were serving.

The last act I did in building the HR division was appointing a manager for organizational development, a job that had not existed at the company.

The new structure divided HR into three clear levels of activity:

1. The operative level: full preoccupation with the level of organizational accountability in which the HR coordinators were the executing force;
2. The second layer consisting of a combination of activity in the area of accountability dealing with recruiting managers, planning intake processes, providing consultation for mid- and senior-level management (including VPs), producing conferences and division events, planning and managing budgets of HR activities in the division, together with activity in the area of responsibility affecting work processes and work culture in the division, while maintaining the values of HR and the partnership in decisions concerning goals for execution. At this level, the HR managers were the executing force;
3. At the third layer, I worked together with the organizational development

Space for comments & insight

manager, the coordinators and the HR managers to promote issues in the realm of responsibility: organizational culture and processes, norms and values, adapting the organizational structure to organizational goals, and initiating steps that would lead to the realization of the goals I had articulated for the three year period in question.

The floatation device principle worked as planned. When the regional HR coordinators failed to meet their accountability, the other layers in the division pitched in and invested their time in helping. When the HR managers ran into trouble, the organizational development manager and I pitched in to help them. The ability of the structure to meet the level of accountability determined the scope of resources for acting at the level of responsibility.

Until now I have described how goals were articulated, for the short-, mid-, and long-term, and how the spaces were constructed accordingly while setting clearer boundaries and creating defined resources in order to respond to the realms of accountability as well as responsibility.

The organizational structure I built also defined the degrees of freedom. My choice not to group the HR managers as a centralized HR unit but rather allow them to be a part of the division they were serving reduced the amount of control and supervision I had over their routine work but it permitted them to actualize their impact in the divisions in which they worked. At the same time, I reduced their workload by transferring responsibility for the operational side of recruitment and new employee intake, which had been part of their previous job description, to the HR coordinators. As a result, they now had new resources of time, energy and thinking at their disposal.

Space for comments & insight

The beginning of the process was extremely complex. The HR managers who had been used to working independently continued to work without coordination and consultation. It got to the point where they would compete for resources amongst each another, and they continued to deal with organizational development without coordination or consultation with the organizational development manager. Their conduct prolonged the separate cultures that had developed in the different divisions and made it impossible to construct a unified company culture. To make it possible for me to manage the boundary between freedom and license, I redefined the process for approving order so that every order had to get my approval before being sent to a provider. Thus, in a simple, practical way, I assimilated the notion that freedom had boundaries.

However, I had no desire to become a bureaucratic administrator, so I made every act of control into an act of consulting. The HR managers quickly learned that that the boundary is not only limiting but also an occasion for learning. They were on the frontlines and all the credit went to them, but in addition they also gained professional knowledge and courage resulting from my own experience and vision for the future. As a result of this process, unified values and a unified culture started to emerge in the division affecting the entire organization. On the one hand, the HR managers and their respective division managers retained very high degrees of freedom; on the other hand, clear boundaries emerged.

The status of the HR managers in the division managements became stronger and their impact was significant. All of this was attained within less than three months after the launch of the new organizational structure of the HR division.

Space for comments & insight

The degrees of freedom of the coordinators were defined in practice in the field. When asked to whom the HR coordinators reported I would usually answer, "To their customers." As I've noted in the earlier chapters, the goals at the level of accountability are easier to articulate because they are immediately defined by the customers, be they external or from within the organization. Any situation that was not fully resolved resulted in an immediate customer response. The coordinators' conduct was predetermined by processes defined together with the HR managers and with my approval whenever I was asked to give it. Communication between the managers and coordinators was greatly based on their personal connection, and in practice what managed them was their body of customers. As a result, their independence was quite extensive.

I used to invite the coordinators to a meeting every two to three weeks because I viewed them as having an effect on the echelon of employees at the forefront of the company, and I wanted to maintain my direct influence on them. I took advantage of these meetings also to improve processes by together studying successes and failures, to add to the coordinators' knowledge of HR, and to connect them to my vision for the company and the division.

Forums — Holding and Containing

The most important forum in which holding and containing processes took place was the HR management meeting, with the participation of the HR managers and the organizational development manager. Of course, the meetings had very concrete goals of handling tasks for the entire organization. Every meeting included update of the managers about their tasks in the division so we could all have a picture of what was happening in the organization. However, the main thrust of the meeting was given to

Space for comments & insight

the tasks of the managers involved in developing the human capital in the company and the tasks connected to the vision.

The first really meaningful meeting took place about two months after I started working there and after I had studied the organization and the division, the organizational sensitivities, and the pace of the changes the organization could contain, and after I had defined the goals and constructed the program to realize them. When all of this was ready, I called for the meeting with the HR managers and presented the entire program to them. I presented the future division of activity by layer and my perception of the importance of meeting accountability fully, even though it is merely the initial base of the function of HR. I presented my understanding of their role, my own role, and that of the organizational development manager. I presented my vision about establishing a country-wide training center and the need to find new ways of recruiting employees independently of external contractors and with more efficient diagnostic tools than assessment centers. Already at this point I raised the need of constructing a computerized system for managing résumés and finding alternate methods for selecting candidates, even though I had no idea how to do this within the framework of the company's limited resources.

The HR managers' reactions were mixed. Some of my ideas aroused great enthusiasm, especially the vision of a country-wide training center. At the same time, they were very skeptical about the feasibility of realizing this vision because of the financial constraints. They were happy about the intention to recruit HR coordinators to handle the daily operations of recruitment and new hire intake, but their joy was mixed with a certain worry about losing control. I assume that some of the worry about loss of control was associated with the fact that I was a Johnny-come-lately manager making changes that would leave them without control; should I fail or simply disappear, they would have

Space for comments & insight

to deal with the resulting chaos I had created. At that time, cynicism and skepticism were organization hallmarks. Changes were so frequent that no one made any effort to assimilate them because another change was sure to appear before long. Furthermore, the company was short on cash and there were constant cutbacks, making it impossible to develop an infrastructure. The company was operating by putting out fires. Three-month plans were considered long-term; when I told one of the managers that building HR in the organization at a state of the art level would take three years, he advised me not to use the phrase "three years" within company walls. The general sense was that executives arrived, stuck their toe in the water, and either fled or were let go. On my second day with 'yes', the HR manager at headquarters saw me hanging a picture and asked me, cynically, "So, you're here to stay?" During that meeting, reflected in the faces of the HR managers, I could see the distrust that any long-term program, requiring fundamental changes and economic investment, would ever come to fruition.

An important part of my task was to establish trust that the goals and the vision were realizable, to hold the vision and contain the doubts and anxieties, some of which were a direct result of the vision and some of which were derived from the feeling that the organization was experiencing too much turmoil and too many changes.

Containing the doubts and opposition was also not easy. The doubts were grounded in reality and it was wrong to treat them lightly. The challenge I set the division and myself was not simple at all, but at the same time I can say that I had a fairly clear mental picture of what the organization would look like once the goals had been achieved. I put a great deal of time and thought into the stages I would have to go through on the way there. I was reasonably certain that it was possible to succeed.

Space for comments & insight

Routine meetings with the HR managers hardly touched on operational issues or follow-up of performance, but rather dealt with the organizational culture and education. I usually left the performance and assimilation in their trusty hands. I gladly and often shared my knowledge and varied experience to enrich their understanding of the space in which they operated. I dealt very little with details and a lot with essence, and I hardly ever used the authority vested in me by virtue of my title, exerting instead my professional authority. I was not considered a strong manager, but as a simple fact I set very ambitious and significant goals for the organization, and I am proud to say that almost all were achieved. It is my belief that the goals were attained because the space I built for them allowed it to happen.

One day I brought a glass bowl to my office and filled it with candy. The candy disappeared rapidly, but from time to time someone would bring in a treat and restock the bowl. I used to use the bowl as a metaphor for the importance of space. Even when the space is empty, it calls out, by its very existence, to be filled; were the bowl absent, there would be nothing to fill.

Of course, I owe a large part of the success to other people: extraordinary HR managers who worked hard, built and with great creativity realized all that could be achieved in their space; the organizational development manager who worked with me; Nava Horen who with an strong hand led the process of assimilating the company's values, an extraordinary project; Hayit Skornik Levy who led projects of executive training and fascinating conferences for the large management forum as well as the project of restructuring the field sales force which I describe next; Ofrit Kahana who managed HR of the customer service division and assumed the job of VP of HR when I left the company; and Orit Peretz, director of the 'yeschool' who led its establishment. At the end of the day – or even in the middle of it – the contribution of these women

Space for comments & insight

in the division to the realization of the vision and meeting the goals was tremendous, but to make it happen I was required at all times to hold the goals and the vision and to present them as a reality taking shape right in front of us. I was required to contain a great deal of frustration and opposition from the team and a great deal of self-doubt and my own fears.

Meetings of the HR managers continued to be difficult during my entire tenure with the company. The roots of the doubts and the culture that had permeated the company during its first years were so deep that a constant holding of the boundaries and goals was required; there was constant conflict over managing the degrees of freedom. There was a constant fight to break the boundaries. At the same time, a new language was created in the HR division – the language of the vision. The company was undergoing a process of assimilating new values and fascinating processes of organizational development. Value-laden and ethical boundaries were forcefully assimilated under the leadership of the CEO who brought with him a broad worldview of business management that allowed for the space in which the parts of my vision, which had to do with the organizational culture, could be realized and exist.

Another forum I maintained was the forum of the HR coordinators. This forum had a number of goals, many of which were routine and concrete, such as solving problems and improving working procedures, professional consultations and also adding to the coordinators' knowledge of the HR field. But the central importance of the forum was as a bridge for affecting the conduct of junior executives and employees in the field. The assimilation of values and norms does not take place in fancy ceremonies or through repeating slogans, but rather in the daily decision making and conduct regarding the smallest of issues: how and when to allow an employee to take vacation, how and when to rebuke an employee, and how and when to help

Space for comments & insight

an employee with his/her private issues, how to welcome a new hire and how to let an employee go, what you do when an employee is homebound for several months because of an accident at work and is not receiving a salary any longer, whether or not to deduct the salary of someone who is ill but has no more sick days, how to deal with an employee who wants to leave but wants the severance pay to which s/he is not entitled and therefore refuses to cooperate with her/his superiors, how to deal with an employee who committed a traffic offense driving a company vehicle, and on and on. The coordinators' field of activity brought them into daily contact with the norms of behavior of the employees and the team leaders at the company's different sites. When the forum met with me, we would raise these issues and discuss them, as well as look for solutions and processes of assimilation and influence that were in line with the goals and boundaries I had set. These meetings were critical for assimilation because meeting the people in the field over and over again eroded all the new learning and the meetings had to shore it up and re-assimilate what they had learned. During those meetings I was able to contain the frustrations of the HR coordinators and strengthen their ability both to hold the normative, value-laden boundaries and contain the frustrations of the employees and team leaders.

The third forum I used to assimilate the culture, norms and values was a forum that was created by chance thanks to an organizational change. As I mentioned at the beginning of this chapter, at a certain point in its existence 'yes' operated out of three separate locations, each of which was managed by a CEO. Several months after I assumed my position there, the company transitioned to a country-wide management format and the regional CEO positions were cancelled. Each of the regional CEOs was appointed VP. The obvious question was who would be the manager responsible for each site? At every site there were managers in technical division, the sales division and

Space for comments & insight

the customer service division. At the company management meeting several alternative scenarios were examined, one of which sounded natural and legitimate, namely: the most senior executive at the site would be the site manager. To me, the solution seemed fraught with error, because the tendency of the manager would be to make decisions that suited only the division to which he belonged. It is important to remember that the boundaries of resources are usually very rigid – the physical space of a site, the budgets for construction and information systems, training rooms, and meeting rooms. It is only natural that tension surrounds the boundaries of such resources. I proposed that the sites would remain without a top manager but would rather be run by a management team in which all the members were equal, a sort of site management forum. Fortunately, Ofer Bloch, the CEO, accepted my position and put me in charge of operating these forums.

The senior sales, service and technical support executives of the sites participated in these forums, as did the site Housekeeping manager and HR coordinator. Discussions in these forums touched on welfare, construction, security and administration.

Once a month, the Administration Manager of the company and I would join a meeting of each of these forums and listen to the problems they had been unable to solve on their own. These occasions gave me a unique opportunity to affect the organizational culture, relationships and employee welfare in a direct, unmediated manner. This mechanism allowed me to hold the boundaries and contain the organizational anxieties, frustrations and anger.

A very important part of the vision holding processes was its gradual realization. Without a gradual realization, the vision loses its impact and influence over the space. Every step of realization contributes to the belief

---

Space for comments & insight

that the vision is possible. The first part of the vision to be fulfilled was the establishment of a national training center. Other immediate achievements with regard to the budget and the status of HR in the organization turned the profound skepticism I had been confronting into cautious belief.

Managers and employees fell in line with the requirements under the influence of the HR division, whose employees became the company trendsetters. The people at HR were supported in the holding and containing processes. That daily support assimilated the vision into the company's perception in terms of the vision's language, timetables, boundaries and degrees of freedom. The success of the people in the field and the sense that they were, in fact, having an effect gave rise to additional initiatives and ideas.

I will not go into the details of how the goals were achieved, as the purpose of this story is only to demonstrate the management model of building space with its attendant physical and psychosocial components. My job was to build and manage the HR space, to create goals, and to hold onto them until their realization, to create boundaries on the one hand and freedom on the other, to contain all the anxiety, jealousy, anger and aggression and neutralize their destructive effects through work, and that is what I did.

When I undertook an employee poll, one of the things we looked at was the company VP's management strength. Most surprisingly, and mostly because I had never thought of myself as a strong manager, the marks received for the strength of management in the HR section were the highest in the organization. I do not attribute the success to my own personal charisma; it is clear to me that the survey revealed the strength of the space I managed to create: a clear, strong space that gave people room to actualize their human capital.

Space for comments & insight

I shall now turn to a case history that demonstrates how the intentional construction of boundaries, especially boundaries of ethics and behavior, and the construction of a containing mechanism resulted in the immediate improvement in the functioning of the field sales force at 'yes'.

The sale of services at 'yes' Satellite TV was carried out in a number of channels, the primary one being its door-to-door sales force. In the period under discussion the competition was very tough. On the basis of market studies, 'yes' knew that its product was considered better, and therefore had no intention of cutting its prices. This stance required a tough fight over customer loyalty, and the salespeople were finding it hard to meet their targets.

For their part, the sales managers tried to promote sales in every way possible, especially by tough management. The difficulty in meeting targets, which resulted in low remuneration and harsh attitudes, had a tremendous effect on the sales reps and the percentage of those deciding to leave was climbing. In order to make up for the relatively low yield of customer produced by every sales rep, substitutes for those who were leaving were recruited, and the total number of sales reps increased. As the result of the demand for rapid and extensive recruitment, the sales forces had to compromise on the suitability of the candidates, so the newer sales reps were a worse fit for the job than their predecessors. This, of course, led to another decline in yield of individual sales reps and the sales force as a whole, another drop in the average salary, and more pressure and aggression on the part of the sales managers.

There was great creativity in the sales management; this was manifested in several new sales promotions, unusual prizes and bonuses, additional conferences, and created a positive, challenging environment. But in practice this meant that every new client sale had become more expensive. The scope

Space for comments & insight

of sales fell short of what was required, the turnover of sales reps grew, and the cycle continued spiraling downward. All the changes and solutions applied by the company were of the "more of the same" type – more bonuses, more conferences and more prizes.

As VP of HR at the company, it was clear to me that the change needed was of a different magnitude. I stated that the system had to undergo a fundamental cultural change. My understanding was that everyone in the system was busy managing results, whereas no one was managing the road to the desired results. To my understanding, the system had lost its boundaries, and the goal was the only parameter of importance existing in the space. It was clear to me that the entire system had to undergo a sort of value-based restart. What I am saying is in no way a criticism of those who managed the sales force in the company. The sales and marketing division was extraordinarily qualified and successful by any measure, and was considered *the* school for sales in the communications field. 'yes' owes the division a great deal for its boundless determination, creativity and resourcefulness. Nevertheless, it is necessary to consider that sales divisions are almost always the initial source for organizational anxiety. By the very nature of their task, the goal articulation of sales divisions is always closest to the level of organizational accountability. Their job description doesn't allow for a time-out for reassessments. A VP of sales cannot stop for a breather and say, "Well, we're now going to stop selling for the next two or four weeks, and reorganize the system." Still, the sales division decided on an organizational shakeup in order to change the organizational culture in the system and make it into a more supportive one. Symbolic of the change in culture, the sales management decided to change the jargon employed in the company, and move away from the military jargon that had been in use, replacing it with terminology from the world of sports. The sales force chief manager was from now on to be known as "the captain

Space for comments & insight

of the varsity team," regional managers would be called "managers," the team leaders "captains," and the sales reps themselves "players." The belief was that the new terminology and structure would serve the goal of changing the atmosphere and the values.

By dint of impressive, methodical work, the language used in the system became more supportive within less a month. Many managers were replaced, and the organizational structure was altered. But a few months into the process it became clear that the results did not meet expectations. Yields continued to fall and the turnover of sales reps did not abate. Despite the change in language, no learning had taken place and no new culture had been instituted. Managers' responses to difficulties continued to be harsh and destructive; their inability to contain the hardships of the sales reps, their own troubles and those of the company as a whole, represented a non-adaptive mode of coping.

At the same time, the organization was undergoing a general process of constructing a scale of values. I therefore took the opportunity to suggest that the pace be stepped up somewhat, and that a focused, concerted effort be expended on the sales force. Fortunately, I was given the mandate to try. One of the things I have learned in life, and my experience with the sales force only reinforced this view, is that change in behavior must take place through behavior itself, not through frontal learning, and I therefore asked Ari Scheleff, from Scheleff Consultants, an expert in consulting and training through role playing and theater, to help out and take part in the process of organizational intervention.

At the first stage, several meetings took place with the field sales force management in which the force's values were identified on the basis

Space for comments & insight

of their manifestation in the daily routines of the division. Values are usually thought of as positive, but as I pointed out in the chapter about boundaries sometimes values are negative, so it is important to identify them. The process of identification was difficult, but very effective. Both positive and negative ones were identified and examined. Among these values were:

- Meeting goals at any cost.
- The unimportance of people as employees and customers.
- Disrespect for general social norms and values.

The next stage in the process was identifying the values we wanted to preserve or adopt as opposed to those we wanted to eradicate or counteract. The final choice boiled down to:

- Meeting goals.
- Human dignity.

Ari Scheleff, along with HR Manager Hayit Skornik Levy and the sales force training manager Devorit Raphaeli, planned a day and a half long business theater workshop for all the managers in the sales division. Different encounters taken from the daily lives of the sales "players" were presented – interactions with customers, meetings with "captains" and "managers" – as were interactions between "managers" and the "captain of the varsity team." Each situation was presented according to both sets of values – the existing ones and those that the field sales force wanted to adopt. The process allowed the participants to transition from the stage of talking about values as boundaries to a behavioral and emotional registering of them as such.

Space for comments & insight

The workshop was extremely successful. Participants left feeling moved. Suddenly they could see with their own eyes the kind of transformation that was needed. Feedback from the sales managers was outstanding and kudos from management soon followed. It was very easy to be fooled into thinking that some sort of breakthrough had been achieved, but it was clear to me that within a week the effect of the workshop would peter out and things would revert to the way they had been before. The daily routine, organizational pressures and especially old habits are much stronger than the impression created by a single weekend, even a very powerful one. I understood that without a setting and ongoing support that would hold the sales force to the new path that had opened up we would never achieve anything sustainable. The task I had set before the sales division's HR manager, Hayit Skornik Levy, and the head sales manager, Yaniv Orbach, was to build the setting and boundaries representing the scaffolding to support the managers and employees on their new path. At that time, I had not yet formulated the concept of space management, but to use its language I would say that it was clear that there was a need for boundaries that would help hold the new path and absent such boundaries the path would be lost.

This construction process lasted about three months, seemingly a long time. But in practice this time was spent on assimilating and learning the new "language," arriving at insights about the importance of boundaries and their maintenance and management by the managers. The regional managers and team leaders – the "managers" and "captains" of the sports lingo – would meet weekly or every other week with Ari Scheleff, the division's HR team, and with me, and together we worked to articulate the insights from the workshops into concrete boundaries of behavior, real boundaries that could be maintained. At the outset, more than twenty boundaries were formulated. It was clear that too many boundaries were going to be ineffective. I reflected

Space for comments & insight

this back to the participants and asked them to take a closer look to determine which boundaries were real in the sense that crossing them would require that the transgressor – employee or manager – be fired.

After dealing with the boundaries of behavior, the team dealt with boundaries of time and place. A uniform daily routine was constructed for the entire sales force: set hours for getting new customer contracts, and set hours for training and development, set hours for preparing to go into the field and set hours for making appointments with potential customers. Regular hours were set for breaks before going into the field and a regular hour was set for ending the working day.

The HR manager of the sales division and the division's training manager did brilliant, creative work, but I would like to single out, with great appreciation, Yaniv Orbach who managed the entire sales force in tandem with the process of organizational change, and who believed that, in the end, good would come of the process and his sales force would recover. I am not sure that I was able to appreciate his patience at the time, but in hindsight I have to say that it was extraordinary. The new management philosophy was documented in its entirety in book form by the training unit of the sale's division's HR department. Clear boundaries were spelled out; these represented the skeleton holding the structure together, a skeleton constructed of a regular daily routine that was the same for everyone and strictly managed, clear physical territories, and clear rules of conduct, for both managers and employees. Team managers received ongoing assistance from the training unit so that they could adopt the management patterns to the new boundaries and norms. In addition, every exception to the norms and boundaries became an opportunity for learning. There were boundaries that, if transgressed, yielded the immediate response of removing the employee: lying, out of control driving and verbal

Space for comments & insight

abuse meant termination regardless of the employee's sales record. At times, this was extremely painful. The management book of the sales division distinguished between deviation from the boundaries and deviation from the norms. Deviation from the boundaries meant dismissal, whereas deviation from the norms required handling by the management.

At the initiative of the sales division management, the company established a body called the Assessment Committee comprised of division managers and HR representatives. The purpose of this body was to hold a monthly discussion of the employees who had deviated from the norms and examine the possibility of continuing to employ them, on condition they be supported, or, alternately, of terminating their employment. The Assessment Committee served as holding and containing mechanism, and it channeled the spontaneous unreserved responses of managers into a formal setting in which there was no room for instantaneous emotional reactions. Managers were no longer required to cope with aberrant employee behavior on their own, and employees were able to present their difficulties before a balanced committee. Moreover, managers received assistance from the training unit, which was committed to help managers in these situations and improve the functioning of employees in the field. As the new management model – with its values, boundaries, time and place settings, Assessment Committee, and implementation of decisions – was launched, the average yield per sales rep rose by 40%. Sales reps and managers, who had been stuck in a place of frustration and despair, started to believe that some good was happening. Most importantly, the sales force as a whole started to make its very important contribution to the company's success. Turnover of sales reps did not, unfortunately, decrease significantly, in part because of the Assessment Committee, which did not allow sales reps who had failed to meet goals month after month stay with the company.

Space for comments & insight

As I've pointed out before, boundaries are of supreme importance in the functioning of every system, but the essence of organizational effectiveness comes from the freedom that exists within these boundaries. Therefore, the next necessary stage was to increase the degree of freedom of the employees in the division in accordance with their abilities. Constructing the boundaries required that we ignore those individuals who didn't need the boundaries to succeed and to fulfill their tasks, and it was only right to restore the degrees of freedom appropriate to them to these people. However, to do so, it was necessary to improve the skills of the managers. The path to change and organizational development of the division was not yet at its end.

As part of the organizational changes in the company at that time, the decision was made to undertake a fundamental structural reorganization. The sales division was transferred to the company's customer service division, and the assimilation of a new culture and new management constructed its own rules. There was an attempt to continue with manager training, but for a host of reasons it failed and the momentum died out. When I think about it now, it is clear to me that it failed because I ceased to hold the path, and it may be that I ceased because my mental picture, my visual representation, was no longer absolutely complete, perhaps because I was tired. As I ended my association with the company a few months after the structural reorganization, I cannot say anything about the functioning of the division after the change. As I've said before, the sales force is always at the forefront and the battle there is endless. In the short- and mid-range, the organizational intervention generated the results the company had hoped for, and beyond. In the long-term, it is my assessment that it evaporated and disappeared.

Space for comments & insight

The End

As I stated in the introduction, this book is a learning space and I will leave it as such, without any recommendations or conclusions. The fact is that people are abandoning closed systems where the boundaries are clear and sharp and freedom is limited. Challenging boundaries and the constant expansion of personal freedom are things I have always believed in, but when systems are so open and boundaries transgressed it is necessary to build new boundaries and new degrees of freedom rather than remain in a licentious and chaotic world. It is my understanding that the current financial and social crises are a result of cultural and social changes that have led to licence, loss of values, and the lack of valid goals. In this, our current crises differ from the economic and social crises of the 1930s. It is also my belief that these crises will not cease and will recur over and over again because any social, cultural and value-based change brings crisis in its wake. To allow us to confront the cultural and economic dynamics, we have to internalize and learn to work with the basic tools for space management presented in this book. Perhaps at times these tools will prove to be insufficient , but they will always be a prerequisite. This is true of every leadership and every space – parental leadership, political movements, statesmanship, as well as social and economic leadership.

Space for comments & insight

Bibliography

Note: The texts cited by the author are all in Hebrew, whether written originally in that language or translated from English, with the exception of *Human Capital* by Thomas O. Davenport.

Adizes, Ichak, *How to Solve the Mismanagement Crisis*, Cerikover Publishers, 1980.

Burak, Jacob, *Do Chimpanzees Dream of Retirement?*, Kinneret Zmora-Bitan Publishers, Dvir, Dan, 2007.

Kim, W. Chan and Renée Mauborgne, *Blue Ocean Strategy*, Matar Publishers, 2006.

Davenport, Thomas O., *Human Capital: What It is and Why People Invest It*, Jossey-Bass Publishers, San Francisco, 1999.

Erikson, Erik, *Childhood and Society*, Sifirat Hapoalim Publishers, 1974.

Fromm, Erich, *Escape from Freedom*, Dvir Publishers, 1977.

Goldart, Eli and Daniella Dinur, *The Goal*, The Israel Management Center Library, 1988.

Neill, A.S., *Freedom Not License*, Yehoshua Cecik Publishers,

Taleb, Nassim, *Black Swan: The Impact of the Highly Improbable*, Dvir Publishers, 2009.

Taleb, Nissim, *Fooled by Randomness: The Hidden Role of Chance in Life*, Aliyat Hagag Publishers–Yediot Books–Hemed Books, 2008.

Watzlawick, Paul, John H. Weakland and Richard Fisch, *Change: Principles of Problem Formation and Problem Resolution*, Sifriat Hapoalim Publishers, 1979.

www.ingramcontent.com/pod-product-compliance
Lightning Source LLC
Chambersburg PA
CBHW061508180526
45171CB00001B/94